# 2fast2house

oh! map

2018 2fast2house / oh! map books

http://2fast2house.com
2fast2house@gmail.com

ISBN 978-0-9991255-5-7

illustration on pages 96 & 97 by xxxxxx.

all other text and images by
møss høpe ångel except where noted.

The scanning, uploading & distribution of this book via internet or any means without the permission of the author is awesome. Please show everyone this book by any means possible. Pirate other books too while yr at it. Shoplift them from bookstores. Fuck capitalism.

excerpts were originally published in DREGINALD, Big Lucks, the Fanzine, and Working It.

design by møss høpe ångel.

SEA-WITCH
volume three: mare piss superkill
by møss høpe ångel

This book is dedicated to all monsters.

Fuck the police.

## CAST OF CHARACTERS

Narrator (Sara) – Gosh, where to start? Only one of many Saras. Telling this story. She/her or they/them pronouns.

Sea-Witch – A glittering cascade of water that froze in place to be lived in but accidentally ended up capable of true emotion. Precious & needs to be held. Gets cold like all living creatures. ETC ETC You get the idea. She/her.

Meteor (may she lay us waste) – Far away. Loves Girls With Assholes. Flat affect. Probably going to kill us all one day. She/her.

Seventy-Eight Men Who Cause Pain – I hate these guys. Just the worst. Go around being nice to each other so they can pretend they aren't literally hurting every other thing that exists. He/him.

People – Don't exist???? Secretly monsters??? They/them.

D – Chill as fuck stoner chick. Probably not real.

J – Satan-loving spider girl. Probably not real.

Client – Some horny bro.

deadname – Weird one?! Hangs out with Strawberry-Witch and/or Sara. Smells like rainwater. xe/xym/xyr.

Leg-Witch – Literally another witch's leg. One of Dog-Witch's sisters. Doesn't talk much. She/her.

Therapist – One of the people whom the 78 Men Who Cause Pain have deemed allowed to determine whether or not we are allowed to be ourselves. Some of them are bullshit. Some of them are a precious escape route. Most of them are some combination of both. Usually she/her or he/him.

Doctor – One of the people whom the 78 Men Who Cause Pain have deemed allowed to determine whether or not we are allowed to be ourselves. Some of them are bullshit. Some of them are a precious escape route. Most of them are some combination of both. Usually he/him or she/her.

People dressed as rats dressed as angels – I like them. Probably not actually people.

The Thing That Resists Naming – Oh come on. It really probably doesn't want us to call it that like its a name. Idk pronouns? It/its?

Candle-Witch – idk

Eight copies of the sun – Live inside Sara. Seem pretty cool. Fun to play with. They/them or it/its.

A friend from when I lived in Sea-Witch – Gorgeous person. I miss her a lot. She/her

Assholes – As a body part they are among the best. As people they fucking suck. It/its? He/him? Give me some context I guess.

Enemy – I thought I was the enemy. They/them

Some lady – I'm just some lady to somebody else. Idk. She/her.

Police – A bullshit 78men word for that cops bacteria. All bastards. He/him.

Plague doctor – idk you don't really have to know about this its some silly 78men shit. they/them.

Man on stage/Man in the sky/Man in the sky's son – Listen what do you even want me to say.

Angels – An angel is a being who creates light or dark and lives outside of time & legibility. I am sometimes an angel. it/its.

Airless-Face-Witch - Twin of God-Witch. Just really doesn't know. She/her.

God-Witch – Twin of Airless-Face-Witch. Rly into wasps I guess? Sex cult diva. She/her.

Cygnet – Adorable monster. Half of a rat?

Swarm of Wasps – Sexy I guess. it/its? they/them? it's a swarm of wasps u can probably figure out some words to use.

Creature inside of Never – Fill me with your sweetest

Rat god – I am beautiful.

Garbage god – I am sinless.

The living creatures - Live in the woods or something. Seems like they're in their own plot. Idk. It/its.

Felix - They found their body. they/them i think

The ghosts inside of me that want to die - The smell of their death stuck in my clothes. they/them. dead/dead.

Aangels - We are being summoned. You are being summoned. It/its?

ix

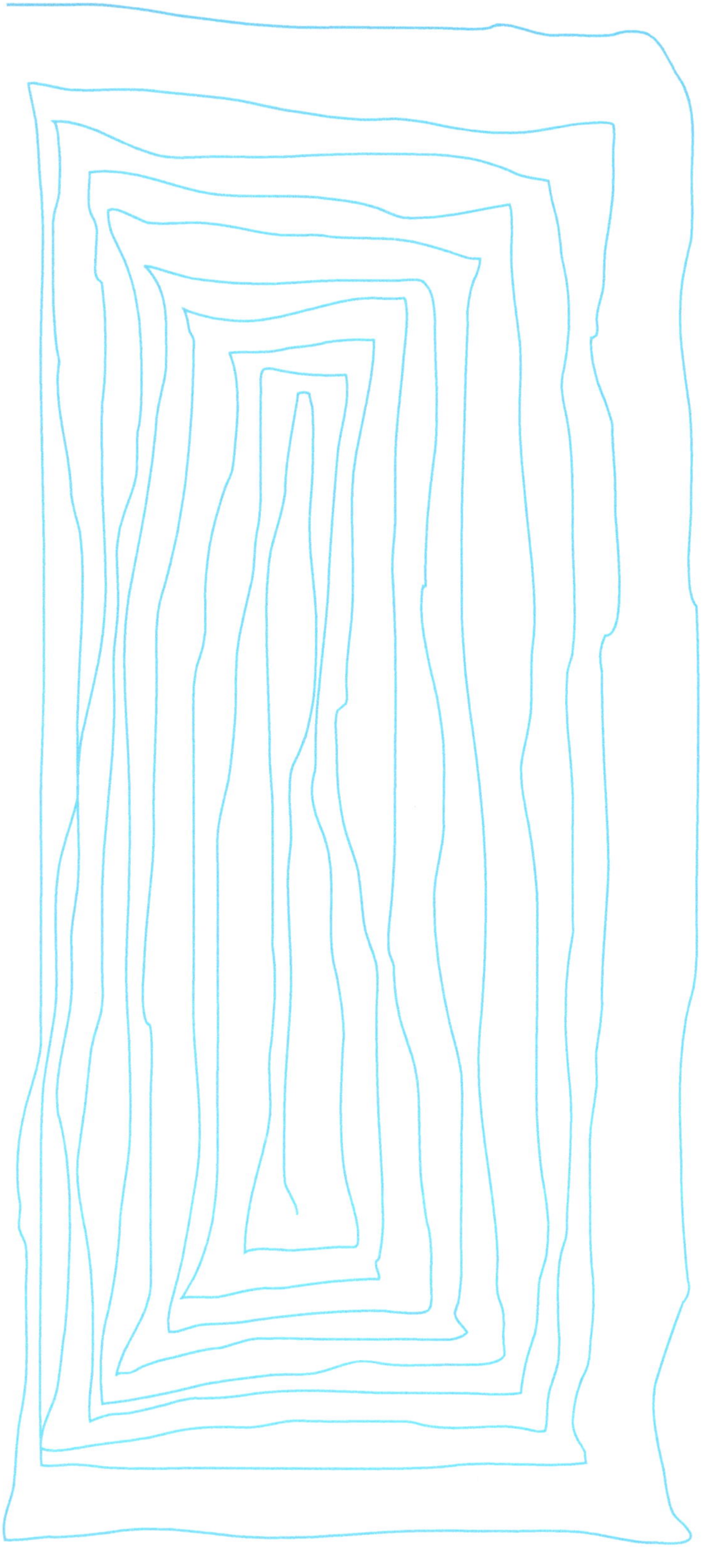

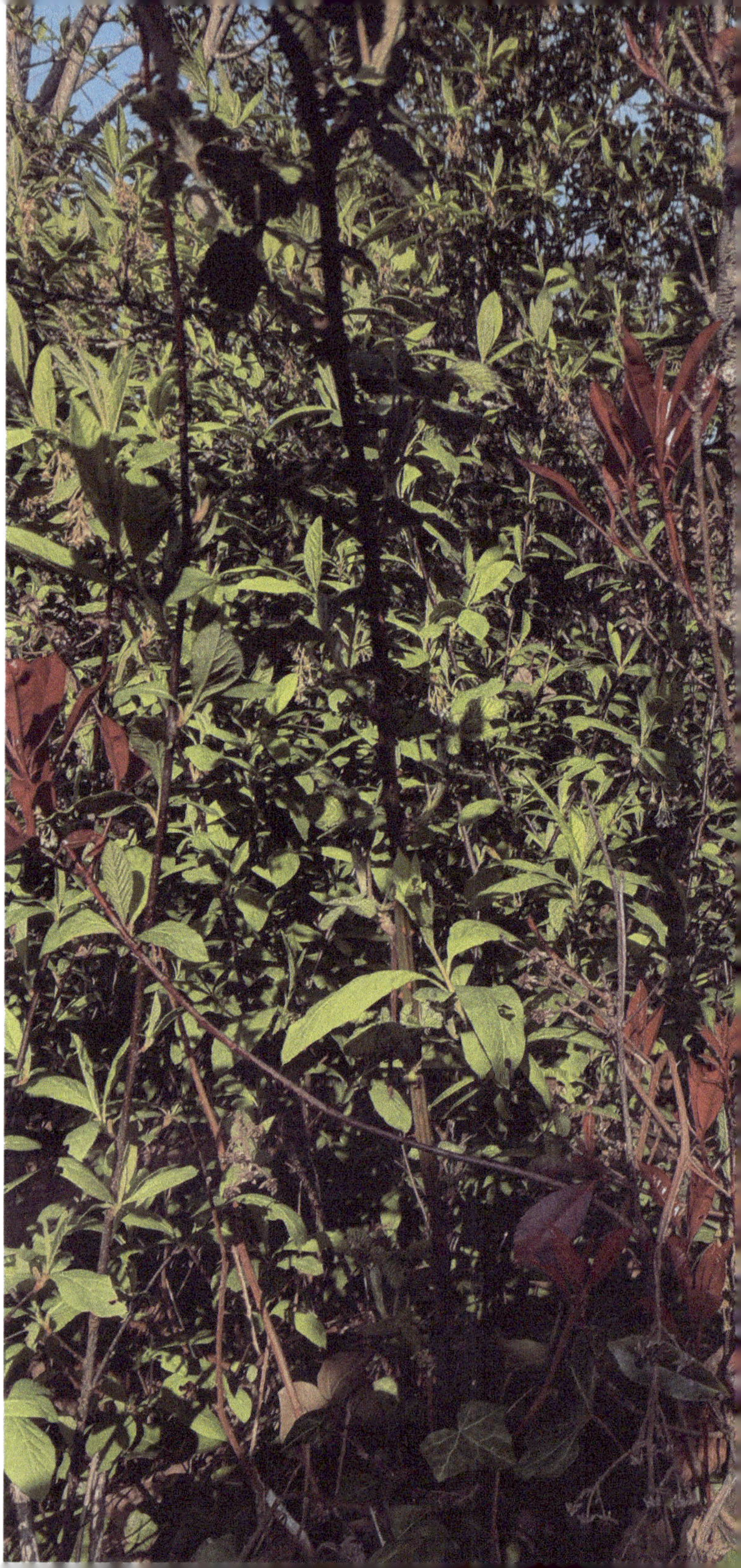

To reach the maximum level
of understanding & enjoyment
you should probably read
volumes 1 & 2 of Sea-Witch
before you read this.


Sea-Witch engages with heavy topics.
This work includes elements of the following potentially triggering things:
sex, nudity, sex work, mental illness, transphobia (including internalized transphobia),
reclaimed transphobic & homophobic slurs, piss fetish, anal sex, panic attacks, sex repulsion,
prescription drugs, suicidal ideation, structural oppression, self-harm, murder, dysphoria,
body horror, unreality.

Please take care of yourself.

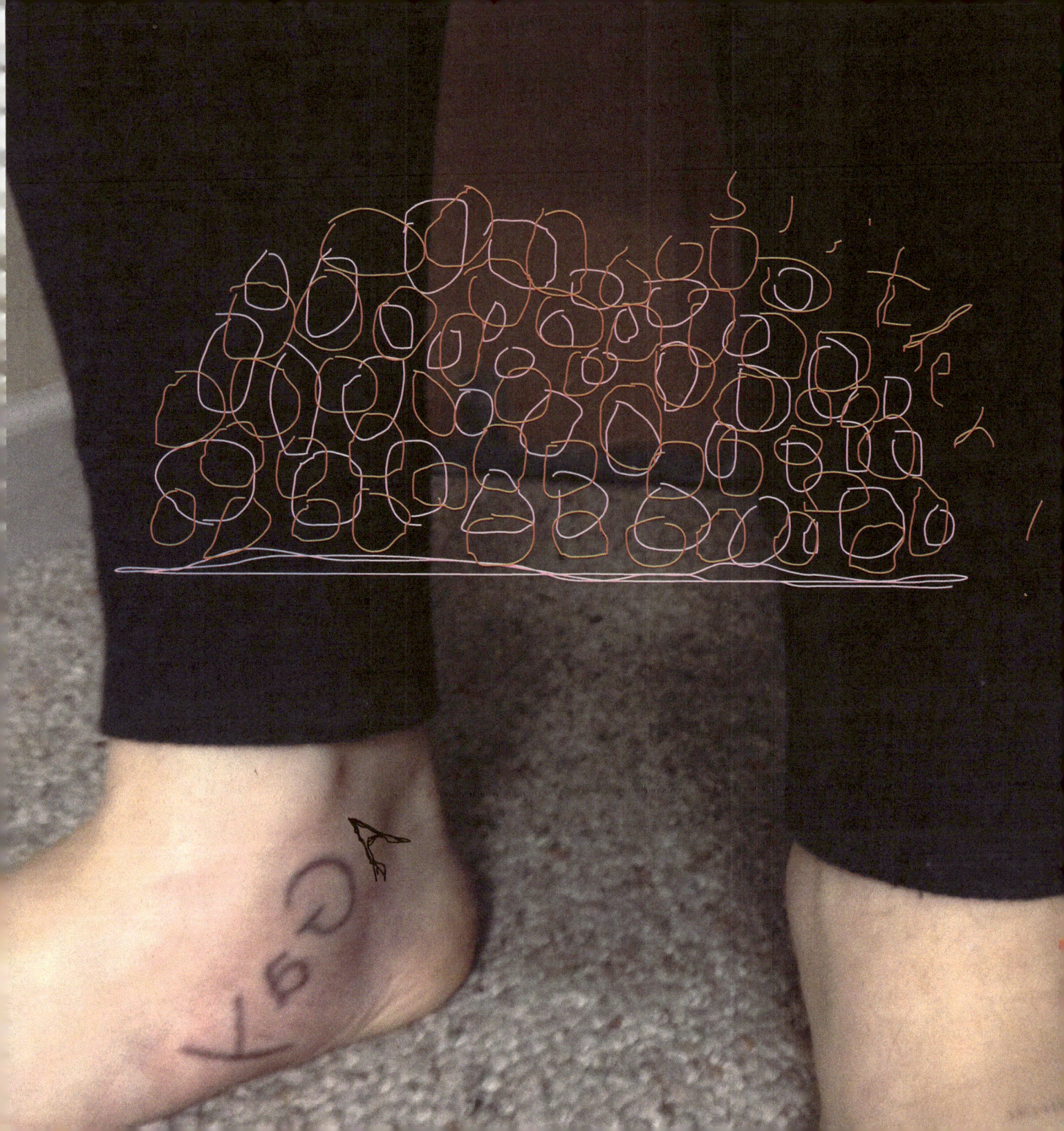

The act of recollection requires particular temporal orienting; this frames the pyramidal neurons to activate in such a way that they become relevant to the body recalling memory. This does not make a memory 'real.'

Experiential reality occurs within a quarter of a second of 'actual' reality; I am never now, here — always nowhere running; remembering;

-Angel Dominguez, *Black Lavender Milk*

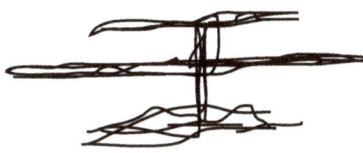

Maybe if it all disappears it doesn't matter
La la la la la maybe

-Talulah Gosh, "Bringing Up Baby"

## SEA-WITCH RAT POWER FUCK TENT 6: COOL SPELLS TO KILL NAZIS

There is a kind of ending that isn't an ending. You see, the 78 men who cause pain can never win. We can win. Meteor can "win". But the ending in which they win is no ending. It is the status quo. They control everything, including us. Well, mostly. But monsters don't need to be born from other monsters. Monsters will exist so long as there is hierarchy that divides by difference. Hierarchy that divides at all.

So for all practical purposes this is an ending. The same way "happily ever after" is an ending. "Miserably ever after." Which maybe means what we should be looking for isn't really an ending at all. Maybe it's a beginning.

This is where my head has been lately. This is what I have been thinking about for the past five minutes as I lay in bed staring at the movie I have been not watching while my wife D lies next to me, packing a bong. I space out for awhile longer. The cool thing about having a trans partner is that she's checked out as much as I am. She gets it. I get it. It happens, idk. It's not a big deal.

My pre-transition girlfriends, my ex-wife, all cis, were always frustrated about this side of me. The part that just disappeared for long periods of time. Just like my parents, teachers and bosses before them. I couldn't help it and I still can't. I still sometimes feel like someone is going to get upset when I come out of a period of dissociation: this sudden, dropping fear that I'm letting someone down. But these days that fear is actually unfounded for once. Having a partner who legit doesn't care if I have to spend some time out-of-body is a Fucking Relief.

I moved to ▓▓▓▓ about three years ago. I like to tell people that I "ran away from home to become a transsexual," which, tbh, is pretty much exactly what happened. I left a city, a job, a relationship, a lot of friendships. Idk, it was hard, a bunch of stuff changed. I barely remember it unless I really think about it. Actually, now that I have some distance from it, it's hard even remembering what it was like ~not~ being out as trans. I remember there was this trans woman I talked to right after I came out and I asked her what coming out was like, and she said pretty much that. That she didn't really remember what it was like not being out as trans. At the time I was astounded. Now I totally get it. Trans is just sort of the water I swim in. It's frustrating water sometimes, but it's my water. It's home.

After the movie ends I kiss D and walk into the living room to see if any of my roommates are around. Lately it's been hard to keep myself from holing up with D all day watching Netflix, so I've been trying to pop into the living room to briefly talk to someone a few times a day as an attempt to ward off that closed-up, beginnings-of-panic feeling. We just moved in here a week ago, to a house of mostly trans people who we had been friends with for awhile already. My sometimes-sweetie J is sitting in the living room reading a copy of *Lucifer Princeps*. I walk over next to her. "Hey there," she says, leaning her head sideways against my hip.

"Heya," I scratch my fingers in her soft hair, "How's Satan?"

"Oh she's doing marvelously. Which makes sense, given all the evil we've got around these days."

"You mean dirty-hooker-transsexual evil or nazi-president evil?"

"Well, both. But Lucy seems like she prefers us at this point. Or at least me," she says, glancing down at the stick & poke on her left wrist. I gave it to her a few nights ago on our living room couch, to symbolize J's personal connection with Lucifer. I met her months ago and we immediately connected over all the important things: magic, weird art, leftist politics, mushrooms & being trans. She is my favorite kind of weirdo: a gentle soul who totally gets everything that is going on around her—and in the world in general—but seems so constantly overwhelmed by it that she mostly expresses it in weird little half-joke Facebook statuses. J has been through her share of tough shit. We all have. We've got a bunch of battle scars, and some of those battles still aren't anywhere close to being over.

I notice a text on my phone. It says "hey sexy," which means it's from a client. I've been escorting for about six months now, but lately that has meant ignoring these texts because, honestly, most of these people just want to waste my time. And I hate having to give a shit when it doesn't seem like it will be worth it anyway. I think I would actually love escorting if I knew every dude that sent me a "hey sexy" or a "u ok w first timers" or a "how much just to lick" text was completely serious and sitting alone in a room with a stack of an appropriate amount of bills in an envelope all ready for me. But unfortunately they usually just want to talk to me long enough to get off, or long enough that I will send them nudes so then they can get off. This time I don't ignore it and I text back, "Hey there :) U looking to meet up? $100/30 min or $180/hr. Outcalls only."

J has been absorbed back into her book, but her head is still leaned on me so I give it another scratch while the response comes in. "Yeah. Let's do 30. I'm at the Rodeway Inn by the airport. Meet me in an hour?" Honestly, I'm impressed. This nice fellow actually wants to meet up.

I immediately text back "I'll meet you in 1 hr. What room #?"

Wow. An actual client. Unfortunately I have hella morning stubble and its 2pm and I am only wearing my girlfriend's oversized Grateful Dead t-shirt, an oversized Black Sabbath hoodie w spiky studs on the shoulders & tiny pink underwear. Which means it's most definitely Gettin' Pretty Time.

I give J's head a kiss. "Well, let me borrow that devil book when you're done with it. I think I'm gonna shower now."

"Mrow! Shower well, you," J says as I drift back toward my bedroom, where D is getting stoned and staring at six second looping Japanese instagram videos of hamsters. "Look at this ham," she tells me.

"Oh my gosh, what a small soft baby!" I say, kissing in her hair.

"Do you want to shower?"

"Did you hear me tell J that?"

"Nope! I just wanted to shower."

"These are the things we do I guess," I said into her hair, punctuated by another kiss. "Also I've got a client."

"Nice," she says.

⁂

A person I hooked up with once told me that the problem with showering with someone else was that generally not much actual cleaning got done. D & I prove that untrue on a daily basis. We mostly keep to task while making room for the occasional interruption of groping and moaning, making out and the occasional bit of dick sucking or ass-eating. We're always like this together. This shower is mostly functional, with only a few brief diversions, and the hot water feels good until it doesn't and then the whole bathroom is muggy and steamy and we both start getting lightheaded so we get out. I feel the lightheadedness pushing on me, my limbs start to feel heavy, so I dry and go in the bedroom, where I flop naked on the bed.

"Oh god," I moan to myself as I feel a familiar horrible warm tingling climbing my back. I've always called these anxiety attacks but I have no idea whether the thing that I call "anxiety attack" is anything at all like anyone else's. I had a psych prescriber once tell me they were psychotic episodes, but that seems like a different thing. Idk. I look at my phone and my client hasn't texted back with the room number. My mind wanders and the blankets near my face feel too close, the room feels too small, too lived-in, too messy. All I can think about is that I have spent nearly 20 hours a day in this bedroom since we moved in, though I guess I am totally making up that number. I feel stagnant and my life feels stagnant. I have been existing and that's it and there is nothing about my life that is in any way sustainable.

On top of that, the horrible country I live in, a country that exists because white assholes like my probably-slave-owning ancestors came and killed and cheated everyone who was here before and now we all go around acting like we deserve to live here, yes that same country, has elected an actual fascist as president and even my white skin isn't enough to help me get a fucking "real" job or whatever other things I'm supposed to have planned out in order to exist and I don't even know if I could do a fucking "job" anymore anyway because half of my days end up with me just like this: staring into a room that all feels too fucking close to my face and crying and panicking and I don't think any employer is going to let me be like "oh hey sorry I'm a fucking nutcase so I can't actually do any work anymore today", just like, whenever this happens. Especially because any job I get I'll already have one strike against me because I'm a tranny mess who doesn't own unripped tights and has stick & pokes all over herself including one on her fucking face, which I actually like, but won't do me any favors in the job market.

Which like, fuck the fucking job market, right? It's a whole scam against anybody who is even slightly marginalized in any way at all and I've always said that I'd rather be scamming my way to a cheap living through art and sex work than get a real job anyway. That is until I get too crazy to do sex work and art. It does seem to be getting worse every year. No doubt about that. I always want to fix things by moving to another city—and I could move—but where could I move that I wouldn't just be doing the same fucking thing: holing up and watching netflix with D and having panic attacks and maybe trying to do sex work or else like worrying that I'll never be able to afford rent and like what if I can't get on food stamps there and they probably hate trans people there anyway unless it's like ▓▓▓▓▓ or some big city where everything is too loud and close anyway.

It's not like I wish I was out partying. I hate parties. So does D. We've bonded over it. And we also both freak out at shows, so live music is pretty much always not-an-option. So far the only thing that makes me feel not-horrible and like I'm dying is making art, and I don't even know what the fucking point of that is. What I want to be some cool artist chick. I mean I guess that's what I already am and it fucking sucks because all I do is panic and cry. Basically this feeling right now is terrible and all I can think about is how much I want to punch my own stupid fucking head in but I am keeping myself from doing that. That is not productive because I have already done that a LOT of times and getting (further?) brain damage is just going to make my life harder than it is, which, look, idk about anyone else's life is like or how it would be if I existed in their bodies, but fuck it, I'm going to go ahead and say my life, at least at the moment, is Very Fucking Hard.

D walks in and sees me crying. "Aw, babe," she says as she sits down beside me and holds me in her arms. I hug her hard and stare up into her face and she wipes my tears off, but the panic is settled in deep at this point so I can't stop crying. D knows this well. She's held me for hours through this. She was with me for the entirety of my 30 hour marathon panic-attack-psycho-whatever that ended with me in the ER. I push my face into her towel-shoulder and let out some good hard cry-growls. I feel cold and spent and scraped out inside and more than anything I feel scared through my whole gross boy-man-girl body and into my bones.

I turn my head to get in a more comfortable position and when I turn my head the room moves around me in a way it shouldn't. Fuck. Why can't I just live in a world that sits still. The too-closeness of everything gets worse and nothing around me seems real. I don't seem real. My brain can't seem to figure out where real starts and made-up begins. D's hair is right by my face and it seems like it's coming out of her head in a way that couldn't really happen. It looks like a computer simulation. I think that it's kind of adorable but am immediately deeply unsettled by the fact that I think it's kind of adorable. I feel pathetic and very very crazy, and it feels like the kind of crazy you don't come back from. I think about Sea-Witch. I am so close to D right now. I look up and brush back her hair. The entrance to Sea-Witch is the ear. I'm exhausted, but I go inside. She welcomes me beautifully & I thank her & say now I must sleep & so I lay down on one of her softest orange beaches & let the waves tell me how to disappear.

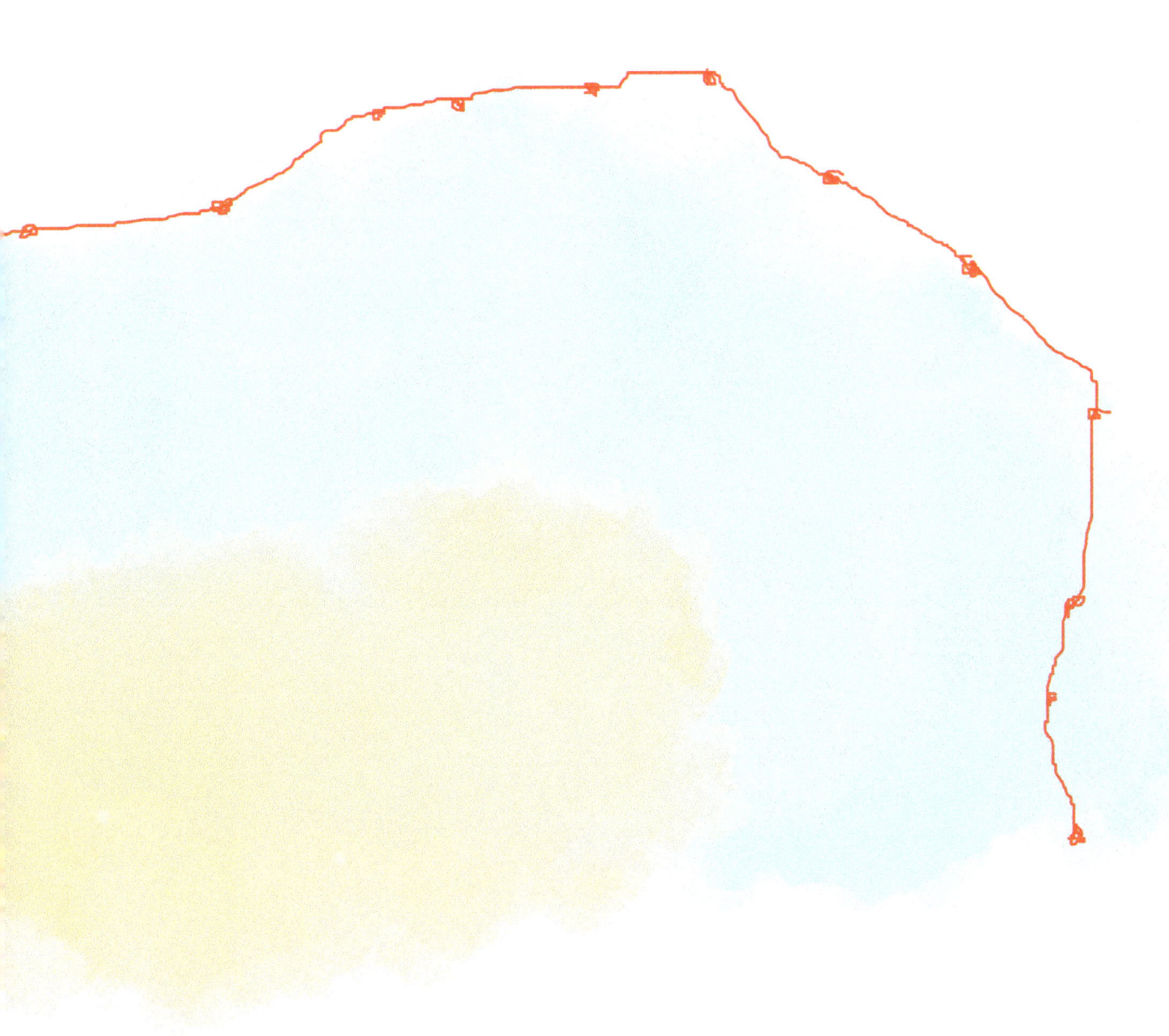

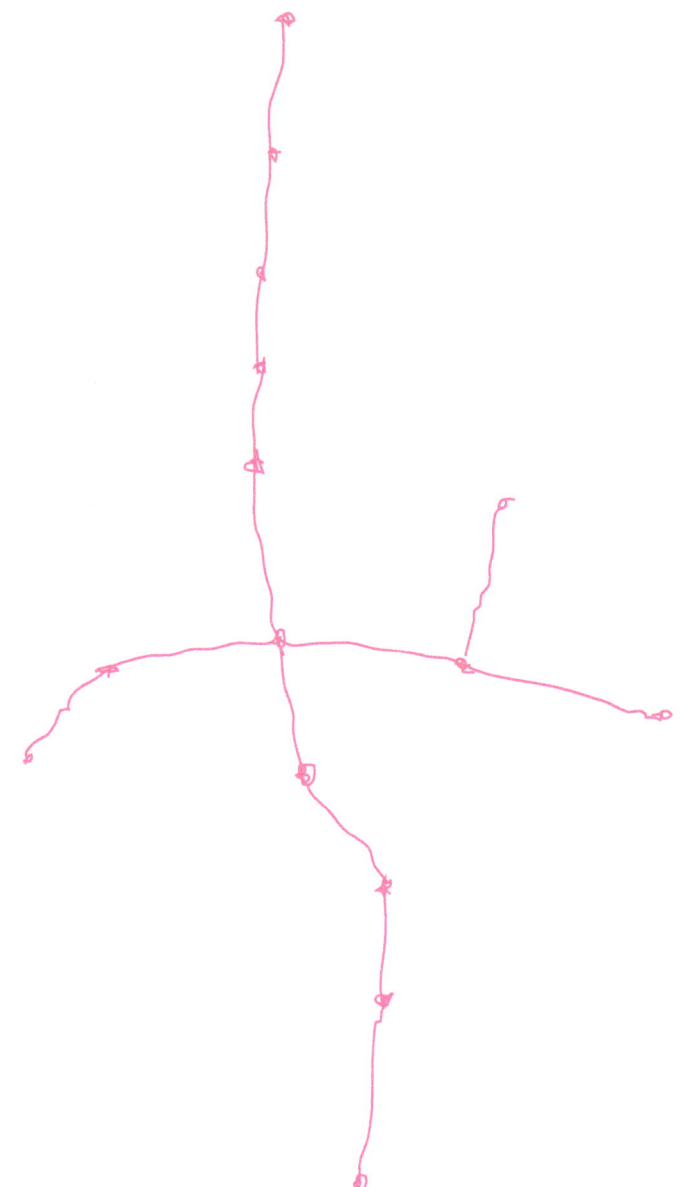

The thing about the apocalypse is it happens to one person at a time. It's an individual experience. My world has Been apocalyzed.

-Dizzy McCallion aka Girls Rituals, twitter post

## TRANS MEMOIR FULL OF GOD

The process of formation, observed from within, is essentially a slow removing of options. Many of these options are options that most monsters have already ruled out, & their loss is not mourned. For example, once one realizes they are a monster it is clear they could never be one of the 78 men who cause pain. This feels pretty okay, ~~because monsters do not want to cause pain~~ ~~because monsters do not want to cause pain to themselves~~ ~~because monsters do not want to cause pain to other monsters~~ because the 78 men seem pretty shitty when seen from the perspective of a monster.

But other options begin disappearing too. They disappear one by one & it isn't so scary really, it isn't so scary until you begin to get close to the endpoint. The endpoint looks like this, & it is two options:

1. Be scared. Be always scared. Be consumed by complete unrelenting terror that seems to have no end.

2. Die.

Option one is impossible to sustain. Option two has so many things getting in the way of anyone actually making it happen that most monsters end up choosing option one as a default. There is a third option, but it feels impossible. Considering this option feels like swimming your way across a whole ocean. But still, it is there:

3. Fight.

The option doesn't say who or how to fight. It just says fight. We need more research. But we are all too weak & tired to research. We fall back into wishing. We fall back into prayer. May she lay us waste.

SEA-WITCH RAT POWER ANAL SERAPHIM<<<1181>>>CRYSTAL LAMENT

Whenever I enter Sea-Witch it is sexual. I'm sure it isn't this way for everyone, but the particular self I inhabit can barely look at Sea-Witch without feeling the downward tug, without disappearing from my own thoughts, lost, thinking about, almost ~feeling~, her hard clit deep inside my asshole, her piss flowing into my mouth, her fingernails scraping the skin on my back. Sex with Sea-Witch felt so literal, but afterward I never knew how much of it really happened. Sea-Witch's sex turns were like this. Their intensity was such that the reality or unreality of them felt beside the point. & so when I entered Sea-Witch this time, she entered me as well.

I took an Ativan. D had been holding me for who knows how long. I kissed her hard. I felt my brain slow down. The word dru g g e d  s l o w l y  worke d  o v e r  me in w a v e s . Thoughts n o  l o n g e r  s t u ck in my head, but just kept get t i n g  p u s h e d  d o wn. I was struck by D's  b o d y  i n front of me. Seeing her s o ft flesh there made the lo w e r  h alf of my body warm with tingling. I wanted to push my face i n t o  h e r  s oft tummy & then I pu s h ed my face into her soft tummy. "Darling!" I half-whispered. "My sweet girl d a r l i n g."

SEA-WITCH JUNE SPIDERLIGHT 3 CLOUDS

Scene: Bedroom interior. deadname & Sara are half-laying, half-sitting on top of the covers in a semi-made bed.

deadname: Okay, can I stop you for a second & ask some questions?

Sara: Sure.

deadname: I just want to make sure I've got things straight.

deadname: So the whole world was underwater. & bears controlled all of the other creatures ruthlessly by using lava. Then Dog-Witch falls from the sky. & manages to steal the lava from bears. & creates land. & forms nineteen sisters, who then spread out & have all kinds of experiences.

Sara: Well, that's what the Book of Meteor says.

deadname: & then at some point the 78 men start doing shit & fucking everything up again.

Sara: Uh-huh.

deadname: & around that time Dog-Witch falls in love with a piece of information & creates Sea-Witch as a being/place of pure good?

Sara: Yes.

deadname: & then apparently Dog-Witch dies at some point. & some of the sisters die? Or maybe they don't all die? Or maybe they do all die?

Sara: Yes, all of those things are true at the same time actually.

deadname: "There are so many dead witch-gods."

Sara: So fucking many.

deadname: Sea-Witch decides to start taking monsters inside her body to protect them from the 78 men.

Sara: Yep.

deadname: At some point you are formed & then you go out & find Sea-Witch.

Sara: Yeah.

deadname: & you live in her & learn about all this stuff & then leave Sea-Witch but also you don't leave. & Sea-Witch is infected with this distrust stuff & also cops maybe? & then there are all these endings that are all different but all real or not.

Sara: More or less yeah.

deadname: Oh also some stuff involving Strawberry-Witch & me & then me & you & then there was someone who worked at a pot farm but I don't remember that whole thing.

Sara: Yeah, me either but I've got it written down somewhere.

deadname: & then also you are living in ~~[redacted]~~ & having panic attacks & talking to your girlfriends & watching Netflix.

Sara: Yeah that's the same story but just told in a different way.

deadname: Oh ok.

Sara: It's a weird version of the same thing. I could tell this story in a million different ways.

deadname: Is it really a story?

Sara: That depends. Like does a story have to have an order or some sort of overall arc or can it just be a lot of things that happened? What if plot is fake?

deadname: I think it can be either. I think plot can be fake.

Sara: Then it's a story. A true story. Not that I believe in truth.

deadname: Me either.

deadname: I'm not real.

Sara: "Real" seems like bullshit.

Sara: Nobody is real.

deadname: Cool. Thank you. For clearing this all up.

Sara: No problem.

deadname: Do you want to fuck again?

Sara: I want to fuck in one reality & don't want to fuck in another.

deadname: I think both of those things can happen.

Sara: Nice.

deadname: Nice.

deadname & Sara split into two different realities. In one of these realities they fuck. The fucking doesn't involve penetration. Mostly they eat each other's asses out & suck each other's genitals until both of them are tired and/or come. In the other reality they don't fuck & instead just read for awhile until deadname falls asleep & then Sara just reads by herself & eventually falls asleep too.

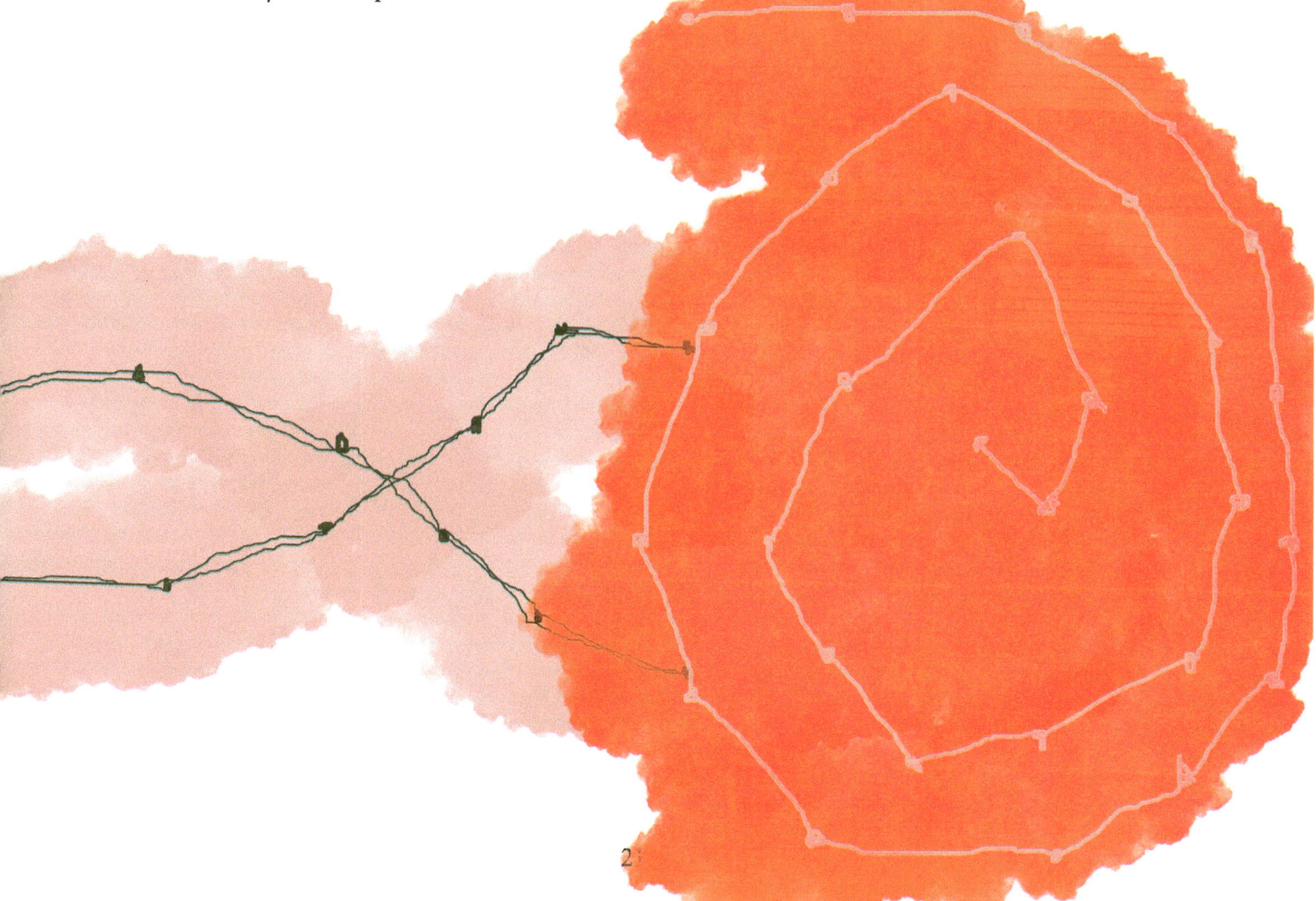

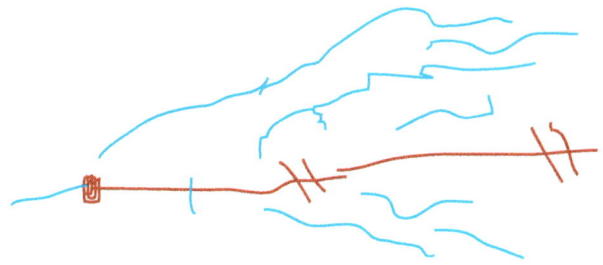

My identity and thus my body are still reflections of my relationship to empire. I can never truly negate my body until this totality is destroyed. But I can gain some level of power in being a monster by choice, and attempt to loose my identity in a legion of darkness. In engaging in total war against civilization.

-Priscilla Genet, *Tomb of Slime*

RAT POWER PDF ALL DEATH 616 HEAL SPELL

I twitch. It's a thing about me. Sometimes I'll go whole days without doing it but usually it happens at least once in a day. There was a while, last summer, when I was twitching nearly every five minutes. I'd wake up in the morning and my first twitch was how I would know I was awake. They start with a feeling of tenseness in my neck or back and then I have to let them out. It's like a sneeze. My head or my whole torso jerks once, quickly, and then it's over. I've told my therapist about these and I've told my doctor and they generally just give me a "huh" and ask me questions to figure out if they're seizures (apparently they aren't) and then they write it down somewhere and that's it, more or less. Given that I'm usually coming to them with a list of much more intolerable things my brain is doing it always seemed like something I could deal with, and I do deal with it. They get worse when I'm anxious or stressed out, but sometimes they happen when I'm feeling totally fine. Whatever it is "totally fine" looks like. Anyway, I twitch. I don't know how relevant this is, but I'm telling you and now you have that information inside you. I think the thing about the twitches isn't so much that I mind them, because I don't, but that they make me feel like a crazy person. When I was twitching all the time every day I was going to psych offices a lot because I was also dealing with a lot of paranoia, a lot of anxiety and depression and this weird thing where I would get overwhelmed and my body would sort of go limp kind of and I'd start slurring my words. Anyway, I was in waiting rooms a lot, sitting there twitching, and I just felt like some hacky casting director had been like "Hm, for this psych waiting room let's have some people who are visibly crazy. I know, get me a tranny wearing a frumpy old sweater that's too big for her and just like, twitches every few minutes." It made me feel like a sideshow. Which I'm already susceptible to, being trans and all.

SEA-WITCH 8 MOUTHS 10000% FURRY BLOG CONTENT NO POWER

I am in a room. There are mirrors lining the walls. There are three doors ahead of me. They have signs on them. The sign on the first door says TASTE OF PISS. The sign on the second door says TASTE OF CUM. The sign on the third door says BOTH! BOTH! BOTH!. I almost enter TASTE OF CUM, but I stop myself. I check myself in the mirrors. I back up four steps & turn. I enter BOTH! BOTH! BOTH!.

Beyond this door the walls are heavily stained. The room smells of lysol. I see two people dressed as rats dressed as angels guarding a door across the room. I say they are "guarding" but I don't know what made me think of them as "guarding". They do not have weapons that I can see. I walk to the middle of the room & look up at the ceiling. In the ceiling there is a grate. I begin to worry that choosing "both" was a mistake. That choosing any door at all would be a mistake. I look into the grate. It is a grate.

"Don't worry," says one of the rat angels. "No one is going to dump piss or cum on you without your consent."

I relax a little bit. I think again.

"What if I want them to?" I ask them.

"I'm sure we could arrange something," says the other rat angel in the least flirty way possible.

I say a quick prayer to someone who is not meteor. Meteor has never minded us having other gods. Meteor understands her limitations. In the Book of Meteor it says "Hey look, I get it. Sometimes you want total destruction. Sometimes you want something with a little more nuance. One girl can only do so much." The thing I pray to isn't a thing I have a name for. It is a thing I have felt & have tried to name in different ways throughout my life. It is a thing that resists naming.

Ok. So.
There are a few things that could happen next:
    1. A flood of cum & piss from the Thing That Resists Naming could come from above, through the grate, & cover all my body.
        a. The rat angels could join in.
        b. The rat angels could not join in, but enjoy watching.
        c. The rat angels could not join in, & feel weird about watching & start talking to each other instead, or kind of stare at the floor & feel awkward.
    2. The rat angels could come over & fuck me.
    3. No one fucks. What is this obsession. Just calm down everybody. I go through the next door, guided by the Thing That Resists Naming, who is not particularly fond of the fact that I have turned its resistance of naming into a name, or that I will probably acronym it later into like TTRN or TTTRN or something.

What actually happens next is some combination of those options. What actually happens next is the realization that "next" as a concept is bound by time & linearity & as you have probably gathered by this point, We Don't Have Much Respect for Either of These Things. But narrative dictates events happen, sometimes even in a certain order. & we have pledged to keep narrative holy. Narrative is what we crave above all things. Our minds need it in order to exist. It is how we remain capable. How we can relate to others. It is essential.

I walk over to the rat angels & they open their mouths for me to inspect them. Their mouths are gleaming white & all light seems to come from inside them. I take the 8 suns from my body & compare the light from my suns to the light from inside their mouths. Their mouths are so much brighter. These suns have gotten so old. I put 5 suns in the left mouth, I put 3 suns in the right mouth. It is the world we have come for, they tell me. <u>Nothing</u> can be the same again. I have the feeling that everything should be over already. I have the feeling that this world has gone on too long.

I remember a discussion I once had with a friend, back when I was living in Sea-Witch. She said "I think I am a main character in my story." I confessed to her that I have always felt like a minor character. A character who had one small scene early on in her life & yet had somehow continued to exist, far, far away from the main character. A character who has been forced to live out a full life beyond any purpose or utility she might have. A character who was not planned out & has gotten stranger & less useful over the years & years she was never expected to live. A character who has been abandoned by the plot, & yet still progresses through time without any direction or purpose.

"Honestly, that's a gift," my friend replied, "because most stories are written by assholes."

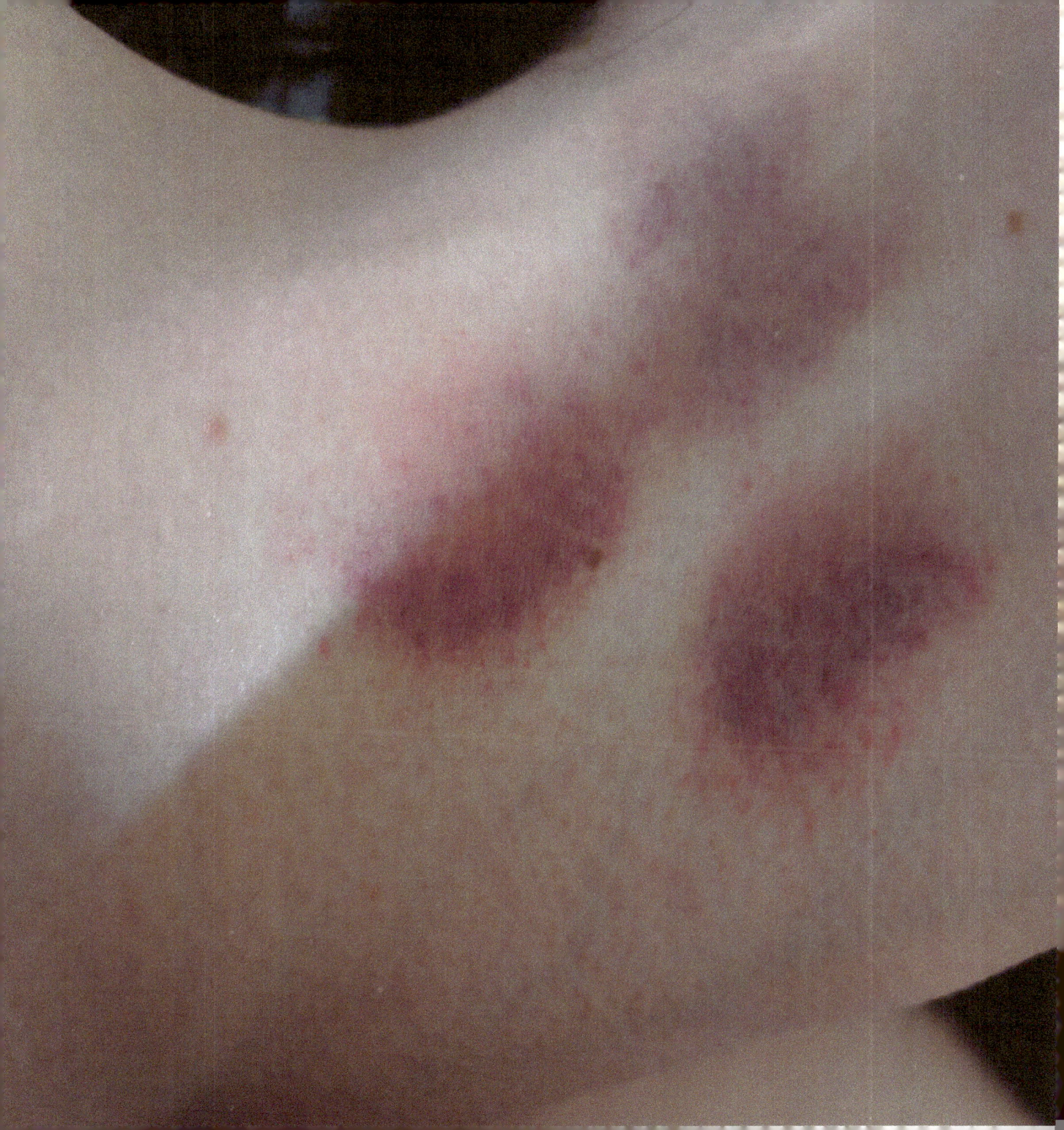

My relationship to my body is neither one of love nor hate,
but rather morbid fascination, as if I'd found a bizarre, dying bug

-Fae Aspen Gehringer, twitter

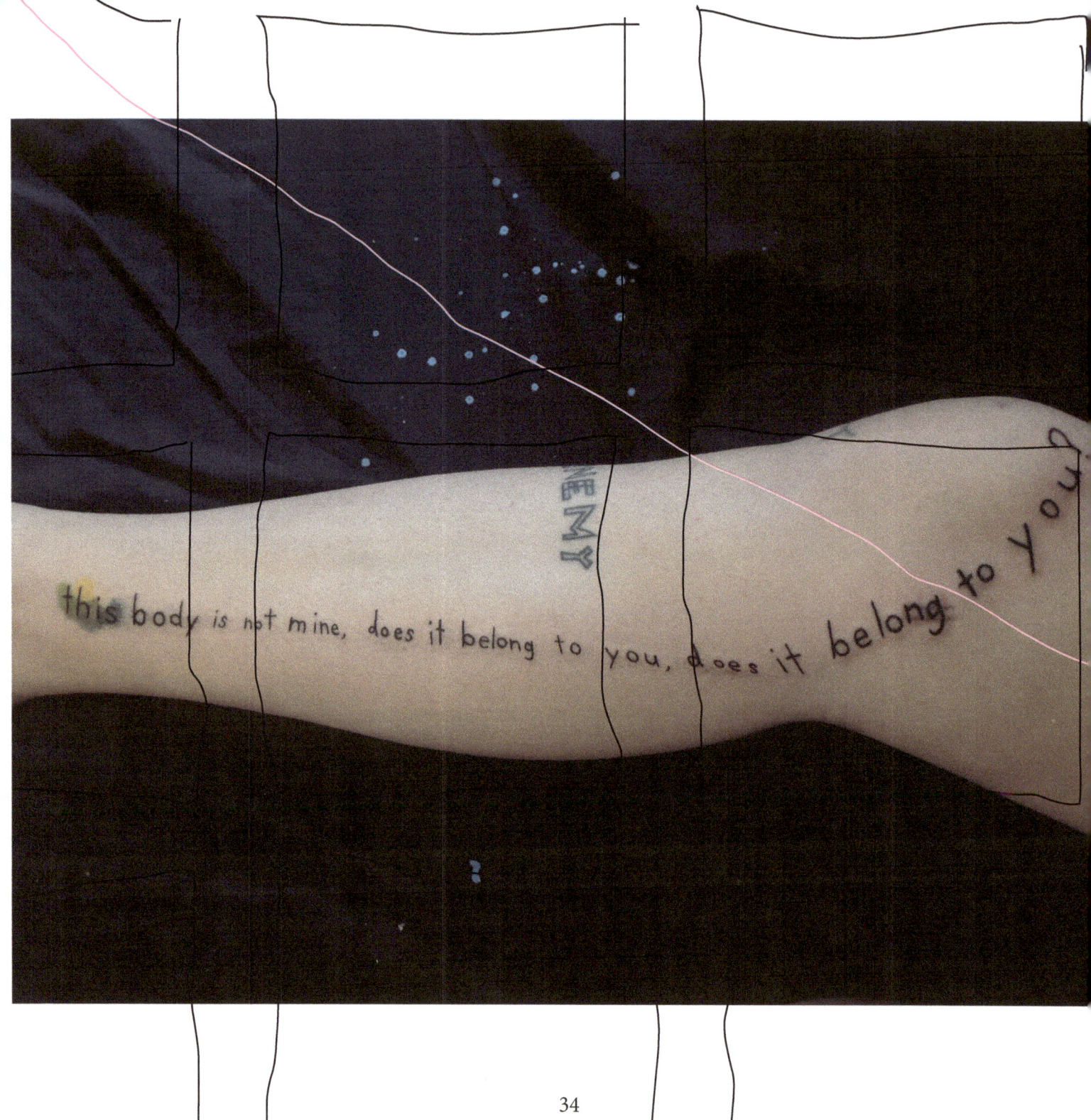

## SEA-WITCH CANDLE-NOTHING WASP-NOTHING 999 RED MATERIAL FROM GOD ABOUT THIS

After I left Sea-Witch, I took a large leaf from the ground at my feet. I used my fingernail & berry juice & a ballpoint pen & wrote a letter to Sea-Witch, but the letter kept shifting its words around the page. I wrote this letter out of joy & desperation, out of a desire to connect with Sea-Witch whom I love. I do not know how the letter looked when it got to her. The first time I read it, it looked different than the second. The third time I read it, it was all marks on a page that held no meaning to me. This time when I read it, right now, before I give it to her, once returning to Sea-Witch and/or realizing I was still inside her, it looks like this:

> When we die, our coffins will be filled with wasps. Those we knew & those we loved, & those we never really knew or loved will come to our funerals & hold their own hands & when they do this their feelings will be filled with wasps. Wasps are made of ghosts, ghosts are made of angels, angels are made of disappointment, disappointment is made of fear, fear is made of control, control is made of power, power is made of ants, ants are made of dying, dying is full of wasps. It goes all the way down. It isn't sequential. Everything is connected & that sucks. It sucks because we want an enemy. It sucks because we have an enemy & he is connected to us. We do not know where to draw the line between him & us. We are full of wasps about this. I pray to meteor (may she lay us waste) & I pray to the thing that keeps me up at night when I am full of wasps (not to the wasps, but when I think of this idea, I pray to them too for good measure). I pray to myself. I pray to my friends. Help me, myself. Help me, my friends. I am all stung-up on the inside. I don't know where I begin as an enemy of my enemy. My enemy does not care where I begin. My enemy destroys those furthest from himself first. Maybe I should do the same. Maybe I should not. I'm too full of wasps & scar tissue to think about this right now. Tomorrow, maybe.

The tomorrow after I wrote this I was not able to understand this more clearly. I must spend further time in prayer to others & in conversation with them (via prayer & not-prayer). I burned myself lighting a candle to pray next to. Sea-Witch told me she did not fully understand the letter, but thought it was beautiful. I told her I don't trust beauty, because my face shifts when I look at it in the mirror. It won't hold still. Sea-Witch told me that this is my secret power. "You have a lot of other powers too," she said. "This is just the only one that is a secret."

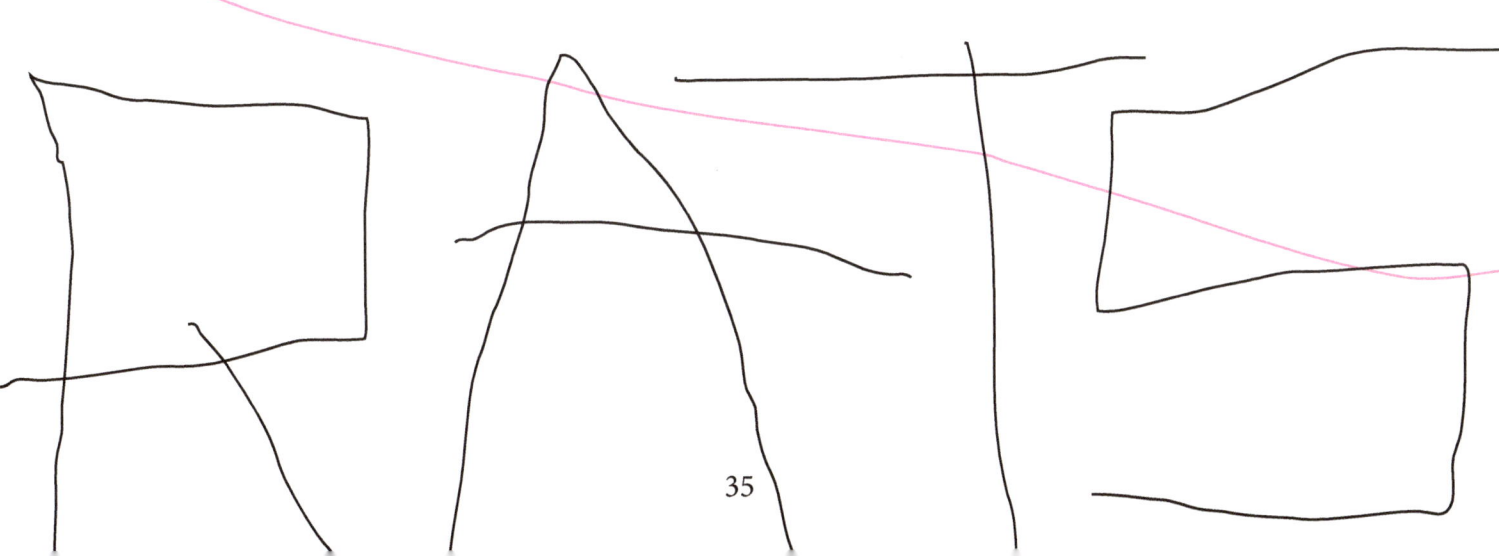

SEA-WITCH ARMOR SICKNESS FULL ANGEL DCXVI

I used to have these dreams where I would be in some big supermarket or some other kind of giant store. Some lady would come up to me & make some horrible comment about how I looked, about who I was, or who I appeared to be to her. I would feel an intense rage building up inside me, & without even knowing I was doing it, I would attack her. She would fall, & very quickly I would realize that she was dead, that I had killed her. I would experience a moment of pure terror. I would become aware of people around me watching, yelling, coming after me, calling 911. I would try to run, but before I could get out of the store there were police & guns & cars surrounding it, coming inside, chasing me. Usually at some point while I was getting shot at, I would wake up.

These dreams were always filled with such strong emotions. The intense rage & desire to let it out. The extreme frustration & horror at realizing that letting it out did nothing but harm, both to the woman who harassed me & to me by putting myself in a dangerous situation. What the stranger did was wrong, but she was a product of her environment. Her horrible, shitty, fucked-up environment.

My reaction to these dreams used to be one where I would decide that violence wasn't the answer. That people didn't deserve to die, that the consequences, both emotional & external, were not worth it. Over time, my perspective on this has changed. Over time I have realized that I just didn't kill the right person.

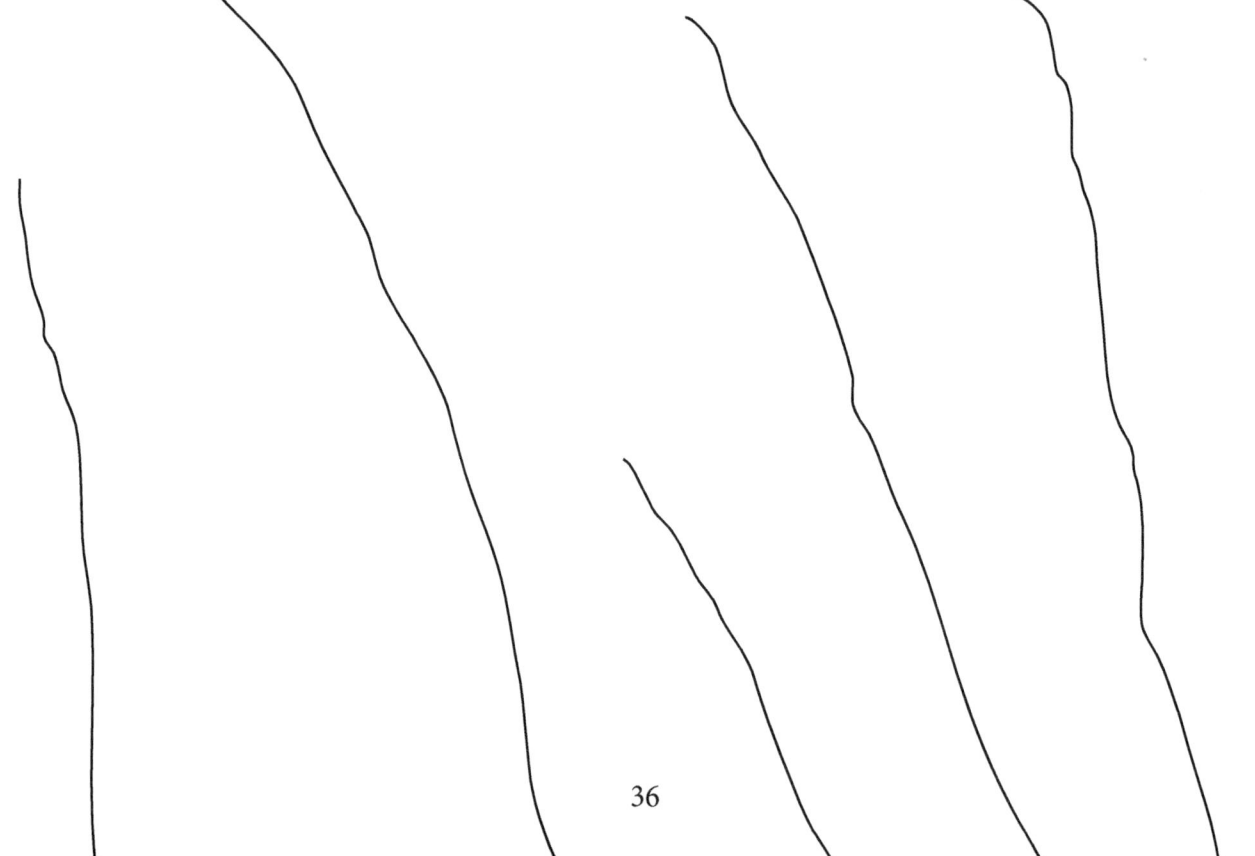

## SEA-WITCH OF PRESSURE BUILDINGS & ALL NOISE: A PRAYER

I hold my face next to Sea-Witch's face. I find the soft skin on her cheek & kiss & kiss & kiss & kiss. I am this creature for you, I whisper on her. I am this creature for you. She responds by pressing her clit deeper against my asshole. I can feel it begin to enter. I am such a creature for you. Yoursoftness,Iamjustthiscreature, I moan against her face. She looks into my eye with both her eyes. I see deeply in the dark parts of her eye & she says nothing as she pushes into me. I am filled with her clit. My god, I say. My holiest god. Fill me with your light. Sea-Witch's hair tickles on my cheek & she pushes into me over & over & over as I feel all the sin leaking from my eyes. I cry the sin out as my god fills me with her light.

we call things by the wrong names but we do our best in trying right?

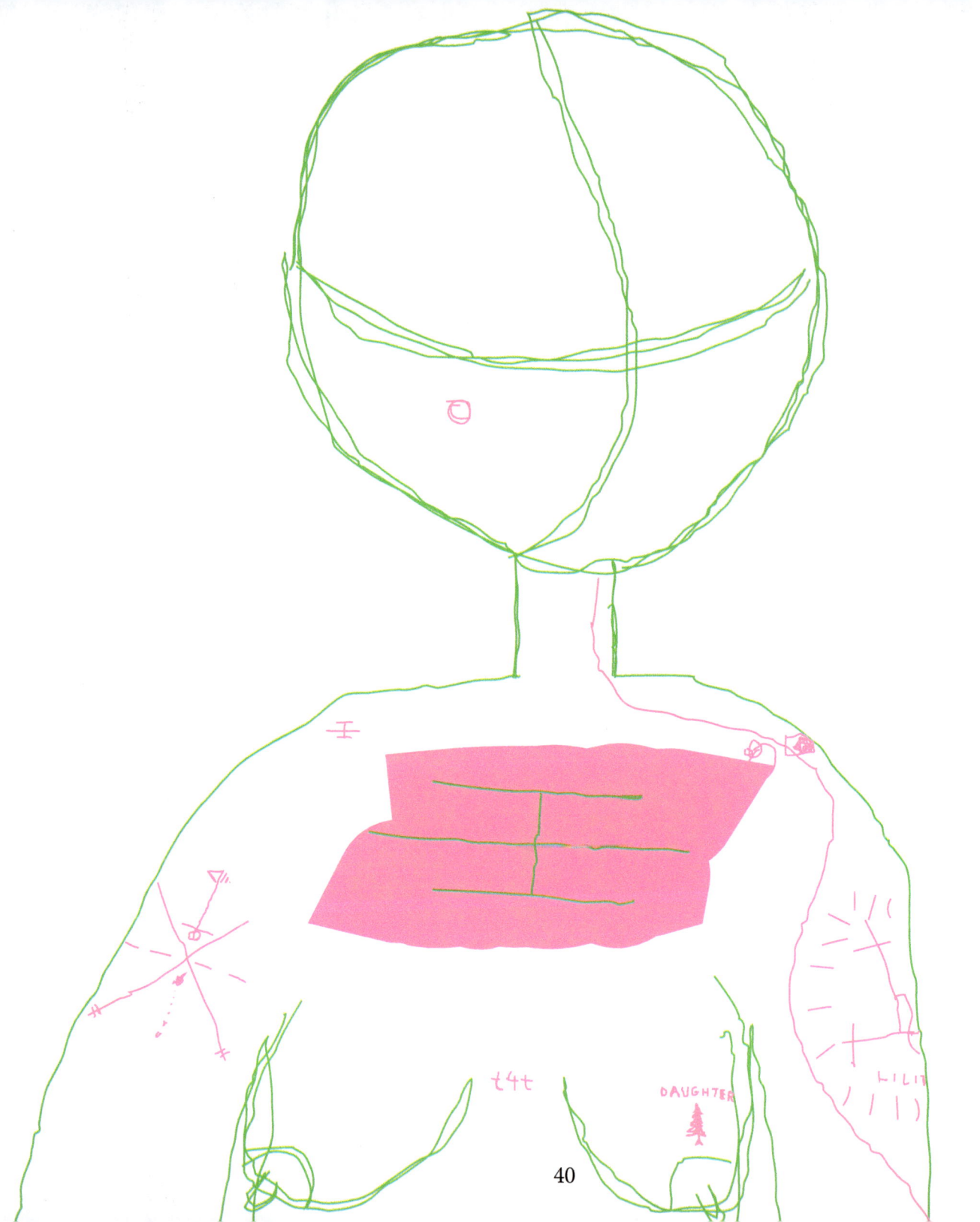

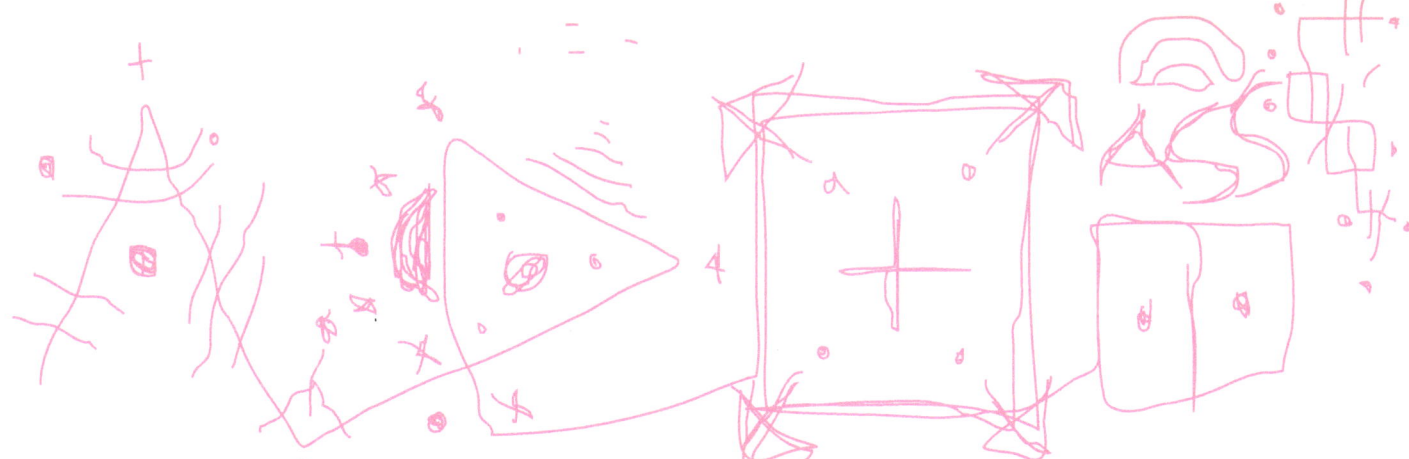

everything leaves, everyone leaves one day but until then it is always i will never leave i will remain here i will forget the passing of time the turning of the sun and the moon and i will grow old here and sometimes that is true and sometimes that is not, we can learn to breathe whatever this is that isn't air and it will pass into our shared circulatory systems and out again only to be rebreathed reversing or amplifying atmospheric concentrations of stuff here inside witch mountain now opened up and pulsing its veins of gold and sunset orange

-Nathaxnne Walker, excerpted from an email to the author

What comes after nothing?

Nothing, I guess.

-Aidan Koch, *After Nothing Comes*

## SEA-WITCH TRANS MEMOIR WHICH HELL WILL YOU CHOOSE TO LIVE IN

Sea-Witch has fallen silent. We do not know what has happened to her but she seems to not be speaking any longer. All of us who live in her are struggling to understand why this has happened. Is she sick from Pain? Is she sick from sickness? Does she have strep? Did we do something to hurt her?

I went to speak to her & she looked at me with understanding.

She has been like this for what feels like too long. We have slept many times & woken to find her in the same state. Two monsters have had breakdowns so far.

Sea-Witch's silence has remained intact. We haven't heard her voice for so long now. The most popular theory is that she has decided this is what she is doing now. Not speaking. Before this she decided to be speaking & now she has decided to be not speaking.

Sea-Witch has held us together. We are falling apart.

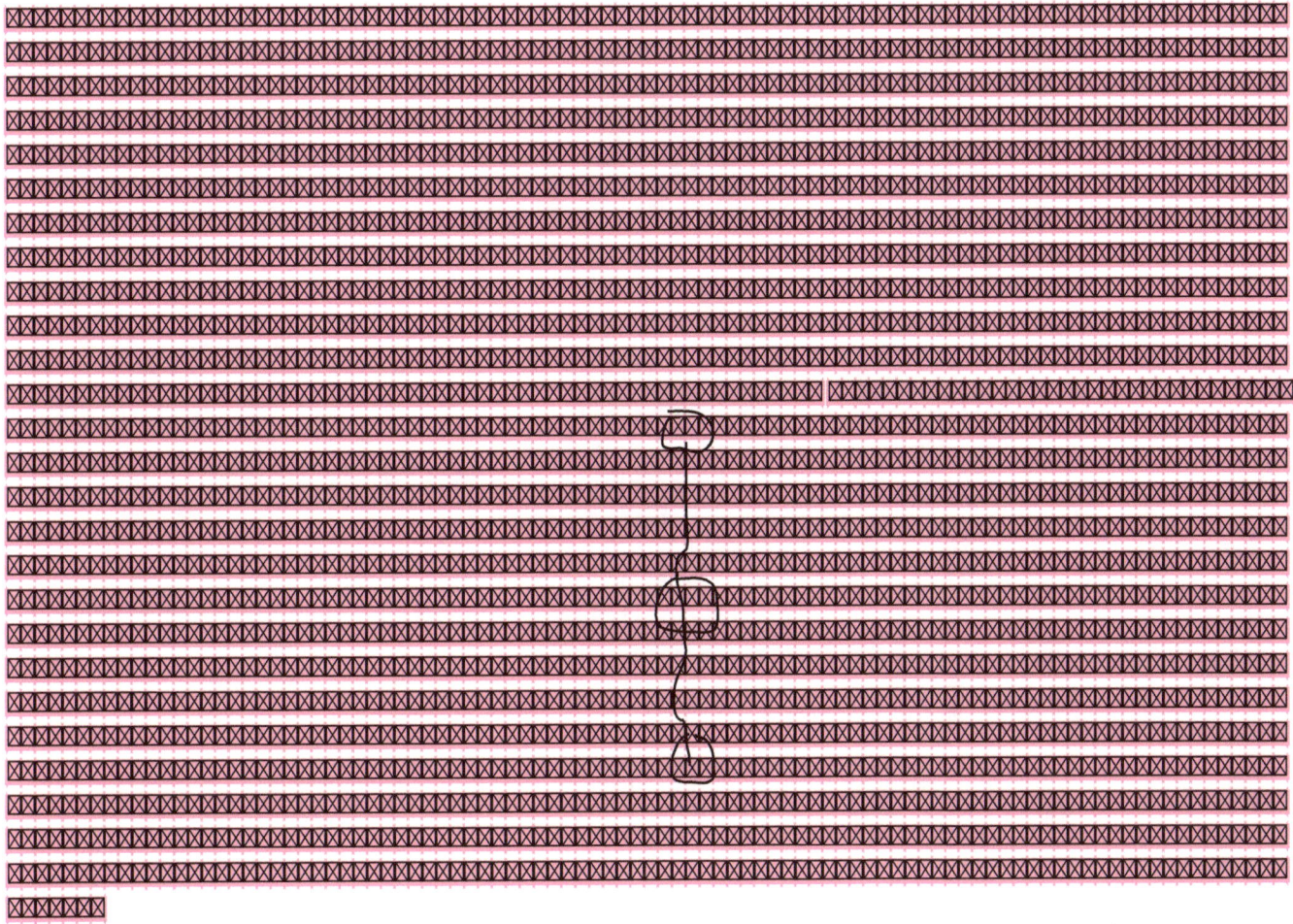

I yelled at another Sea-Witchean. She had been talking about how she wanted to be a person again. The question I wanted to ask her came out too loud. Anger is expressed through volume & movement. I want to be a person too.

Gorgeous sunrise. I am exhausted. I was up all night.

I've been

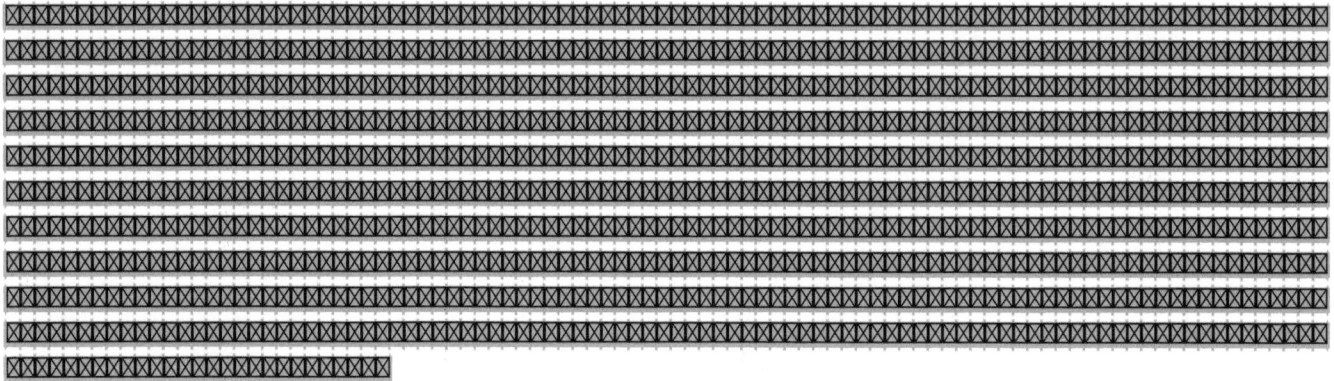

Everything is ongoing. This is where we are. We are deep in ongoingness.

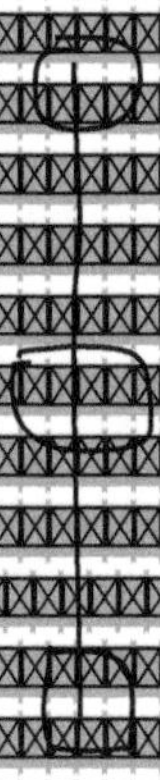

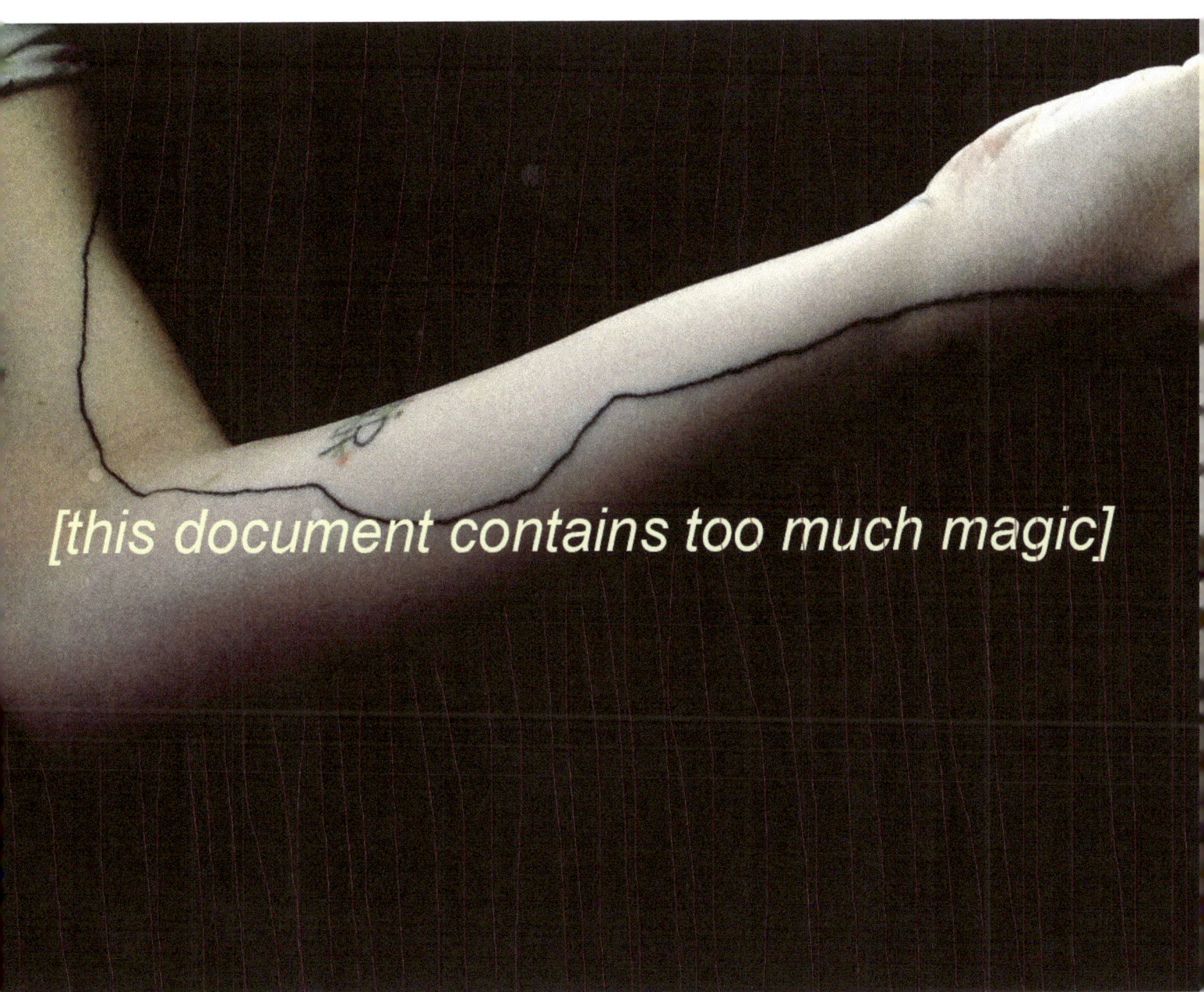

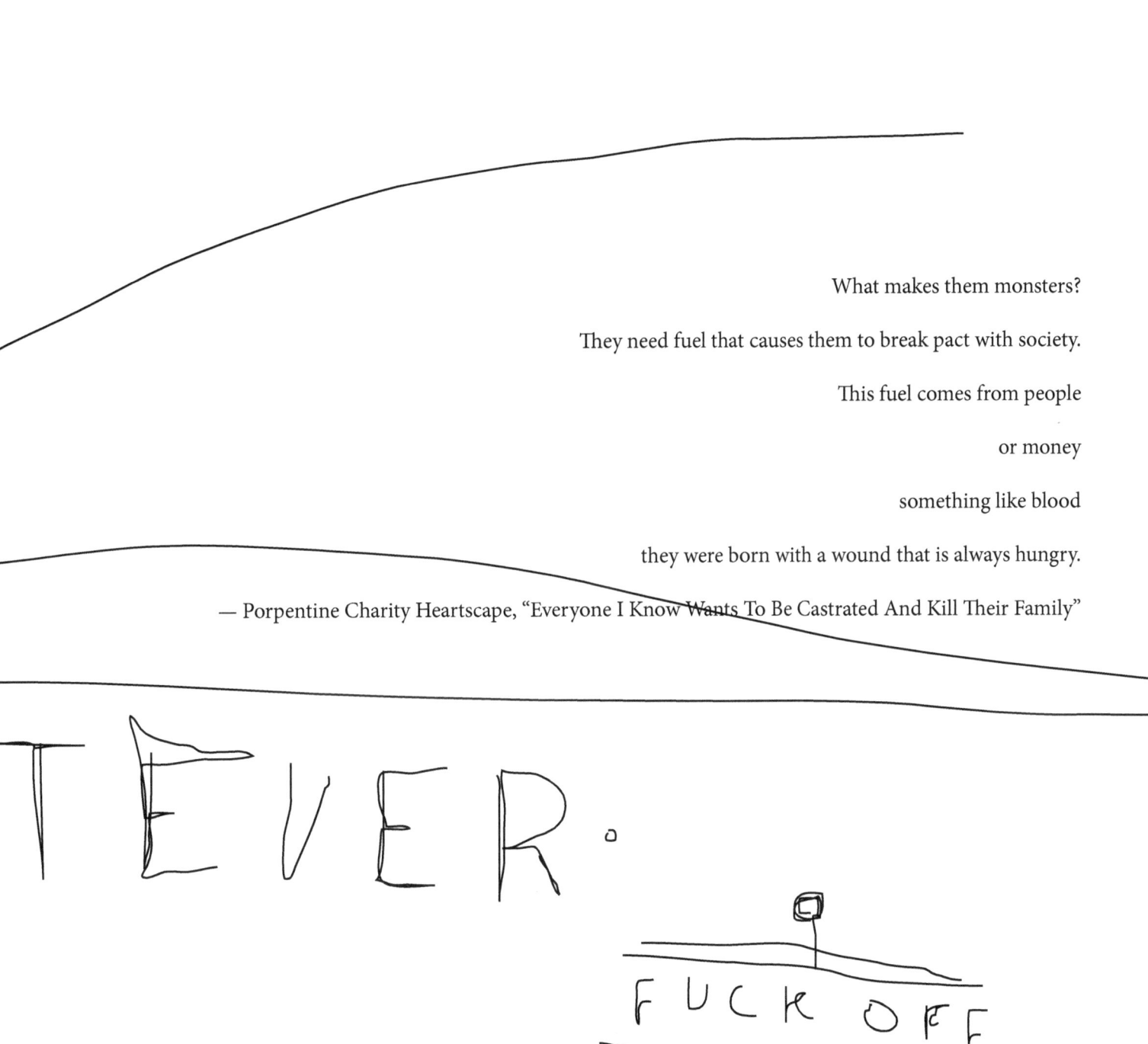

What makes them monsters?

They need fuel that causes them to break pact with society.

This fuel comes from people

or money

something like blood

they were born with a wound that is always hungry.

— Porpentine Charity Heartscape, "Everyone I Know Wants To Be Castrated And Kill Their Family"

SEA-WITCH TRANS MEMOIR THERE IS ROOM FOR ALL THE DEAD IN POISON WORLD

*In this scene I am on the ground. deadname is saying my name. Xe has xyr cock deep inside me & I am writhing. Xe puts xyr hands out & is choking me. I rock my whole body, pressing myself deeper onto xyr cock. Everything feels like pressure & it builds & builds. I am headed for the sun. I can see it in front of me. I feel its heat. Holy shit, fuck me, fuck me fuck me fuckmefuckmefuckmefuckme!!!!!!!!!!!!!!*

*deadname slows & stops. I feel myself pulling away from the sun. I sit up.*
Hey, *I say.* What's up?

I feel...weird, *deadname says.*

Do you need anything? *I ask.*

I don't know, *deadname says.*

Okay. Do you need me here? Do you want to be alone?

Here.

Okay. Do you want touch or no touch?

No touch.

Okay. *The doorbell rings.* Hey, deadname?

*deadname looks up at me.*

If I go answer the door will you be okay here for a little bit?

Yes.

Are you sure?

Yes.

Okay. *I get up & go to the entrance of Sea-Witch (which is the ear). I look in the peephole & sigh. It's a fucking plague doctor. I open the door.*

Hello sir, *the plague doctor begins.*

*I interrupt.* Ma'am.

Oh. *The plague doctor hesitates & adjusts his robes nervously.* Yes, of course. Hello ma'am. I am one of the Plague Specialists over at The Institute of New Pain at the University of Crater & I am here to inquire about treatments you may want to receive as a member of one of our high-risk populations. As you may know, the Plague primarily affects people such as yourself: members of the El Jee Bee Tee Cue Eye Eh Plus community, the disabled, sex workers, people living with mental illness, women, people of color, & many other Minority Groups. I--

But that's most people.

Excuse me?

You said "minority groups" & then listed so many groups of people that you literally covered probably 95% of the world's population.

I sincerely apologize, I didn't--

Anyway, none of those fucking categories are real. The only thing they have in common is that they all Experience Pain.

Which is exactly what I am here to talk about, the Deathpain Plague is--

There is no fucking plague.

Excuse me?

There is no fucking plague. Y'all are trying to fake heal something you started & actively keep going.

*The plague doctor begins to speak in an indulgent tone of voice.* Well, I think if anyone would be qualified to speak on that--

It would be someone like me. Someone who has to deal with this shit. *The plague doctor is flustered.*

Well, that wasn't really why I came here. I came here to see if you were interested in or currently accessing any of our services. We offer a wide--

*I interrupt his sentence by turning my hand into a claw-shape & slashing the plague doctor's throat open. Blood gushes from the wound, staining the front of my outfit.*

[EXTERIOR VIEW OF THE ENTRANCE TO SEA-WITCH (WHICH IS THE EAR)]

*Trailing blood, I drag his limp body inside & close the door to Sea-Witch.*

The door opens & I have tied a rope around the plague doctor's feet.

I tie the rope up so the plague doctor's bloody dripping corpse is hanging above the entrance to Sea-Witch (which is the ear).

I go back inside & shut the door.

[INTERIOR—BEDROOM]

I enter, covered in blood, leaving bloody footprints behind me.

Hey sweetie, how are you doing? *I say to deadname.*

Much better. Thanks for being patient with me.

Of course. I want you to be okay. Do you need anything?

No, I'm okay. I smoked some weed & texted with Strawberry-Witch for awhile.

Oh good, I'm glad.

Who was at the door?

Fucking plague doctor.

Eww, I'm sorry.

Yeahhh. It's okay. He's guarding the door now.

*deadname grins.* Ohh NICE. Fuck yeah! It's been awhile since we had a guard out.

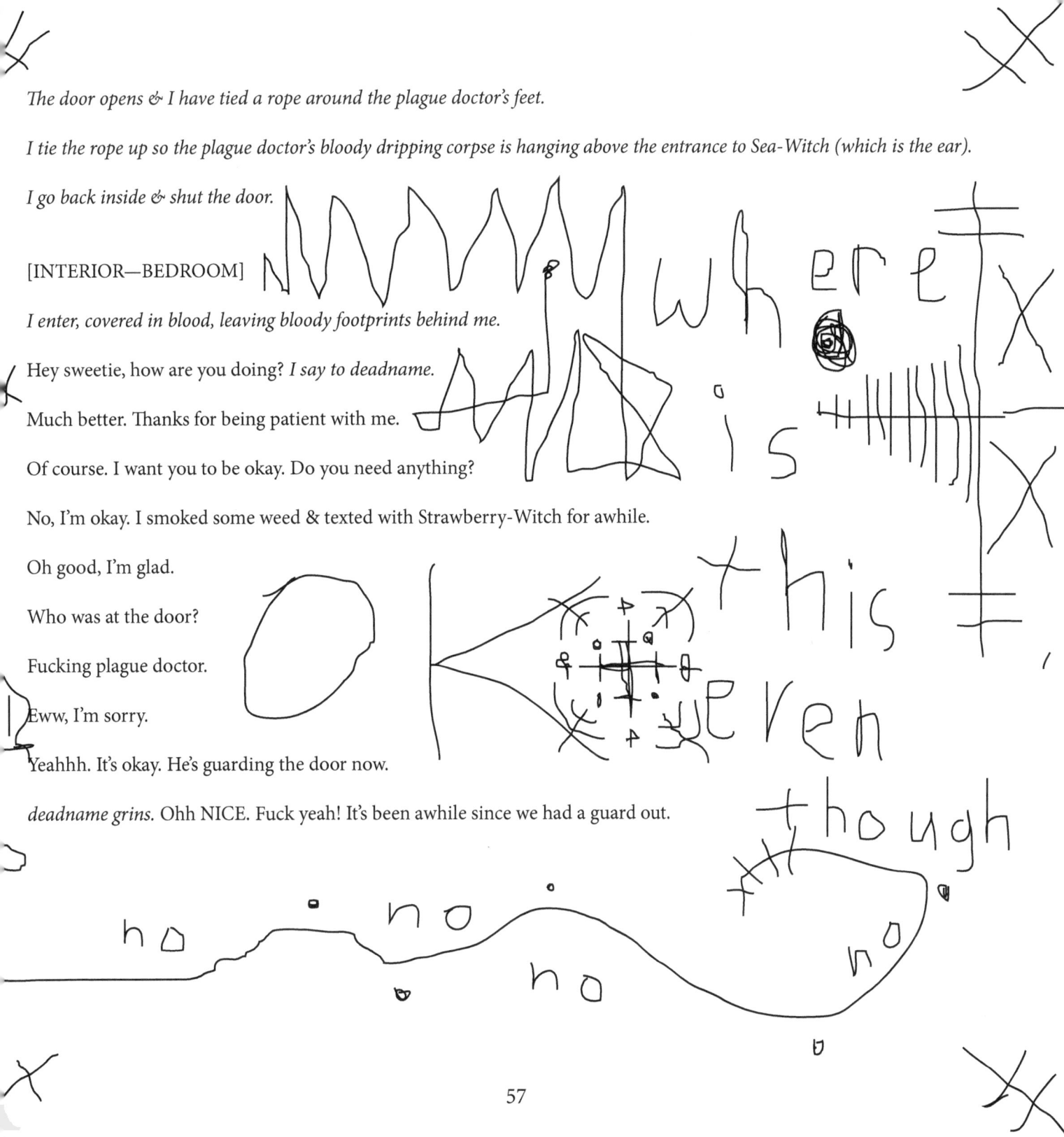

## BONE-DEATH FEVER DANCE 8

Meteor grew up in a house with a nice family. They were nice & so she felt safe & comfortable. Ever since she was small her family told her that there were things that hurt others that she shouldn't do. Meteor decided she never waqnted to hurt others. She found when she hurt others, even accidentally, her family went from being nice to being disappointed & this felt bad. Meteor's family went to church & church was a place where there were songs that Meteor liked, that she was encouraged to sing along with. Church was also a place where a man on a stage would speak to all the people who came to church. The man on the stage talked a lot about a man in the sky who could do anything & decided that the thing he would do is make a bunch of people & then have a son & then get his son killed because this would somehow (?) let the people come to the sky after they died (?) to spend all their time telling the man in the sky how great he is. Meteor sometimes wondered why this was so complicated. If the man in the sky needed people to tell him how great he was couldn't he just make people who only did that? The lady at Meteor's church who taught the children said that god had already done that, & that those people are called angels. Meteor felt sad for the angels. Meteor decided she wanted to grow up to be an angel & go into the sky & tell the man he should do a better job. She decided she would tell him that if he was really so great & powerful, he could make some kind of device that helped him deal with his urge to be told he was great by an enormous number of people & then no sons would have to die & no people would have to live by weird books of rules. When Meteor grew up she found she did not fit in the world of people. People cared very little whether they hurt others, & actually created elaborate systems to do so. & were rewarded greatly for it. So instead of staying on the ground with the people, she did what she had wanted as a child. She became an angel. When Meteor got to the sky it was very lonely. She saw stars & planets. She could not find the man. she searched for him for a long time. She eventually decided that most likely he was back on earth. So she started making her way back there. To all the people & their hurting. She could fix things.

SEA-WITCH TRANS MEMOIR TATTOO OF A BARE TREE SURROUNDED BY RED ORBS

I'm afraid that through the course of this book I might have given the impression that all monsters love one another. It is honestly something I hate & am not proud of & haven't wanted to talk about but I'm afraid at this point I've given you all the wrong impression. Because this could not be further from the truth. Monsters are horrible to each other. We tear each other apart with our teeth & we tell lies so other monsters will join in. We throw each other out in the cold & we play long, manipulative head games over the course of years to ruin each other's lives. We act just like the worst of the 78 men on a much smaller scale. We are horrible, vile creatures. That is what they have made us.

Let me explain. When pain echoes through your head all day, when you feel it as a part of who you are, it is impossible to not get angry. It is impossible not to want to cause pain to others. The 78 Men Who Cause Pain are the rightful recipients of this anger, but they have strategically placed themselves completely out of reach of all monsters. What this means is the following:

1. Monsters want to hurt themselves. When you feel pain, you surround yourself with those who care. When you want to hurt someone & are surrounded only by those who care, who you do not want to hurt, you end up hurting yourself.

2. Monsters usually end up hurting those who care anyway. This almost always means other monsters.

& so monsters spend a lot of their energy hurting other monsters. But we also spend a lot of energy caring for each other. All of the greatest loves this world has ever known were between monsters. All of the most gentle acts of care. We are extreme beings & we act extremely.

I am worried that upon writing this it will become more true. Some of the things I have been writing have been affecting my life. My whole life was torn apart & so I wrote about everything torn apart & it got more torn apart. I am just trying to document but I am afraid this document has too much magic.

lover faggot thief gravedigger graverobber grave lover faggot thief gravedigger graverobber grave lover faggot thief gravedigger graverobber grave lover faggot thief gravedigger graverobber grave lover faggot thief gravedigger graverobber grave lover faggot thief gravedigger graverobber grave lover faggot thief gravedigger graverobber grave lover faggot thief gravedigger graverobber grave lover faggot thief gravedigger graverobber grave lover faggot thief gravedigger graverobber grave lover faggot thief gravedigger graverobber grave lover faggot thief gravedigger graverobber grave lover faggot thief gravedigger graverobber grave lover faggot thief gravedigger graverobber grave lover faggot thief gravedigger graverobber grave lover faggot thief gravedigger graverobber grave lover faggot thief gravedigger graverobber grave lover faggot thief gravedigger graverobber grave lover faggot thief gravedigger graverobber grave lover faggot thief gravedigger graverobber grave lover faggot thief gravedigger graverobber grave lover faggot thief gravedigger graverobber grave lover faggot thief gravedigger graverobber grave lover faggot thief gravedigger graverobber grave lover faggot thief gravedigger graverobber grave lover faggot thief gravedigger graverobber grave lover faggot thief gravedigger graverobber grave lover faggot thief gravedigger graverobber grave lover faggot thief gravedig-

I want to live like that all the time, you know?

Just sharing joy.

I made a patch for my jacket of that one Jenny holzer quote

*In a dream you saw a way to survive and you were full of joy*

I put roses around it.

-Penelope Jeanne Girlblood, excerpted from an fb chat w the author

# BONE DEATH EXCREMENT

God-Witch & Airless-Face-Witch are twins. They are deformed like monsters because they are monsters, but they are beautiful like gods because they are gods. In this scene they are walking down a path in a forest in the middle of who-knows-where. They don't remember how they got there because the sacraments they took made them bad at remembering things like this. They are wearing tiny shirts that show their bellies & underwear without pants. When they walk their beautiful sweat-covered legs whisper through the grass. Insects bite their ankles & with each bite the twins pray to their gods & all their friends. These prayers are wordless, but express thankfulness in some form because the bugs are gods & flesh is a holy offering, or at least this is how it seems to them in this moment because they are super fucked up on sacraments.

They arrive in a clearing where there are two adorable monsters having a picnic. One of them is super tall, with dark skin, dark eyes, dark hair. All of the magic is in her. The other is formless. The other is a ghost. The other is a cloud of vapor. The other is a swarm of wasps. God-Witch gets super turned on by the wasps & sits down against a tree, spreading her legs & taking her cock out & pissing all over herself. Her clothes smell like piss & the wasps come to her, stinging her cock & her face & her curvy ass & her soft asshole as she spreads her legs up into the air above her. Her junk is all hairy & sweaty & covered in piss & she cums super fast.

While this happens, Airless-Face-Witch & the first monster, whose name is Cygnet, stand around awkwardly. It's super weird & so they decide to give God-Witch & the wasps some space. They take a walk. They talk about their friends. They talk about their relationships to other people in their lives. Airless-Face-Witch says that things between her & God-Witch are hard to understand. She says they used to do everything together & there were no questions about it, but lately things have been difficult. She says it feels like everything is on fast-forward & she can't seem to adapt. Like, God-Witch joined a sex cult recently where they all get together & have super steamy hot sex with each other like all the fucking time & she is always talking about this sex cult. Airless-Face-Witch is like pretty down for sex cults but she tried to go there, to the building where the sex cult was & the door was this enormous puzzle. She couldn't figure out how it worked. She tried for a little bit to figure it out & got tired & fell asleep on the porch & then hours later God-Witch came out all sexed up & was like "holy shit that was hot" & Airless-Face-Witch was like "oh sweet I'm glad you had a good time." "I don't know," Airless-Face-Witch said. Cygnet listened to all of this quietly & nodded along. When Airless-Face-Witch was done, Cygnet told her a story. This story had no arc. In Cygnet's story things just happened & then stopped happening. There didn't seem to be any connection between the pieces in the story except that the same names were mentioned. The concrete details of the story seemed false. Parts were overly obvious. There was one part with a sex cult, but the sex cult was a branch on a tree that was blown into the ocean. The ocean took the branch far away. The ocean fell away from the branch & the branch was suspended in non-matter. Time backed up & moved forward arbitrarily. It sped up & slowed down. The story never ended. The story was all endings. It ended twenty, thirty times. Airless-Face-Witch wrote a blog about this story while it was happening. Recapping different episodes. The blog became very popular & then the blogging platform it was on fell into disuse. Nobody reads blogs anymore. Then it never happened. We move in & out of the story like a summer child in the wrong swimsuit, diving, climbing out, diving, climbing out. This child never gets tired. Cygnet changes clothes. Airless-Face-Witch changes clothes. They both change clothes. They take off their clothes and put on each other's clothes. They forget whose are whose. They move in. They fall in love. They have a relationship that lasts two years & then gets complicated. One of them wants to see other people. One of them becomes a rat. One of them doesn't want to date a rat anymore. They forget which one is a rat. I forget which one is a rat. It isn't clear which one is a rat. They see the bodies of people they have never met, being torn limb from limb in a void made of 10000 mph winds that blow in all directions. They cry for their relationship. They cry for the end of the story. The end of the story never comes. They both become a rat. They each become half of the same rat. They live in the walls of a story. They eat the insulation. They eat the insulation. The story gets colder without insulation. The atoms that make up the story grow more still than ever. The atoms that make up the story are harmless. They try on their sisters' clothes when no one is home. They panic when they hear the garage door. They never get caught. The atoms that make up the story never get caught. They come out at 29. Their first marriage was a mess. They made a mess of a lot of things, some of which have to do with that marriage, but most of which are about other things. It's too fast. It's all too fast. The story is falling with no destination. It falls & falls in an arc around a spherical surface that turns at a rate which matches the story's falling. The gravity is immense. The falling happens too fast. Things fall past the story & the story just barely keeps up. It does the things it needs to do to live a life, but just barely. It misses a few, but mostly gets it. It all moves by so fast. It needs a second to rest. The story needs to end.

TRANS MEMOIR STARLIT RAT SCENERY SPOIL CARVE 3 LORAZEPAM
[EXIT STAGE RIGHT, COMPLICATED]

The milk my breasts began producing was clear & sticky. I could place a finger to my nipple & watch the strings it made as I pulled my hand away. The strings would sag, then fall. Another sacrifice. I conceived through my asshole & assumed that was where the child would arrive from when the child arrives. I have heard stories that among Men & People pregnancy happens when a bodily fluid from one is entered directly into the specific hole of another. My hole has been subject to a wide range of bodily fluids, both my own & that of many others. It is no wonder that my belly grows rounder. It is no wonder that I sense that my self is full of a creature not fully myself.

I like myself today. I like my round belly & my hands that rest on it & those hands' markings today. I wonder idly, daydreaming about what creature I could contain. It could be spider or wyrm. It could be dog or liminal thing. It was almost definitely liminal thing. I look at myself, full of cryptid. Full of warmth & chill. I feel full of future. Maybe this being inside me is prophecy. Maybe I will birth a prophecy.

I changed my name last fall. Once I was called Sara, as we are all once called Sara. My name now is a series of shifting signifiers. Both more complicated & direct. The piece of my name I will give you for now is Never. Don't expect this piece to work in other timelines or unrealities, but in this specific realm of unreality I will answer to Never.

And so, as Never, I am to create a Thing that will arrive & gain sentience, possibly. I am to work my muscles & stretch & tear my skin to make way for its arrival.

Why does healing take so long? I did a ritual to the Rat God & at the moment of the ritual where I stated my intention I said why does healing take so long. Rat God answered me but I was not listening to eir words. My skin crept. I should ask again.

This morning I say a prayer to myself as I go downstairs to sacrifice my garbage to the garbage god. I say a prayer to myself as I set my garbage on fire & piss on the fire. The sun in the sky & the suns in my body glow brightly today. I feel their warmth. I feel them passing their bright information to my body & its passenger. Healing. Some day this thing will heal & come out of me. Some day it will let me heal as well. My role here is container. Pitri. Incubator. New words among the other things I have been called. Lover. Faggot. Thief. Gravedigger. Graverobber. Grave. I have a heist planned for this afternoon. Come with me.

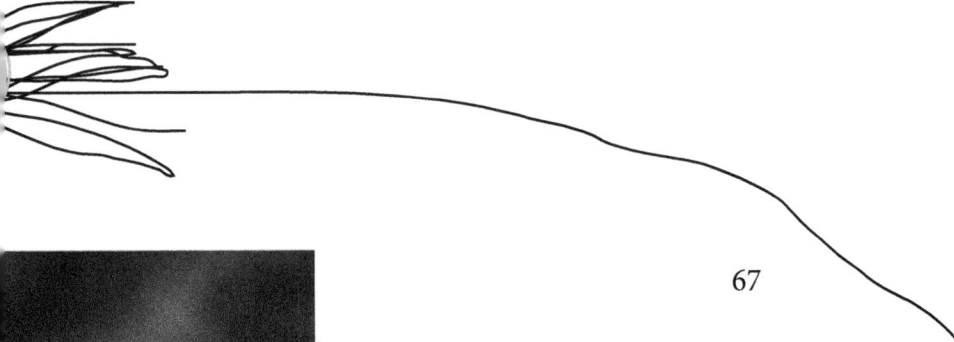

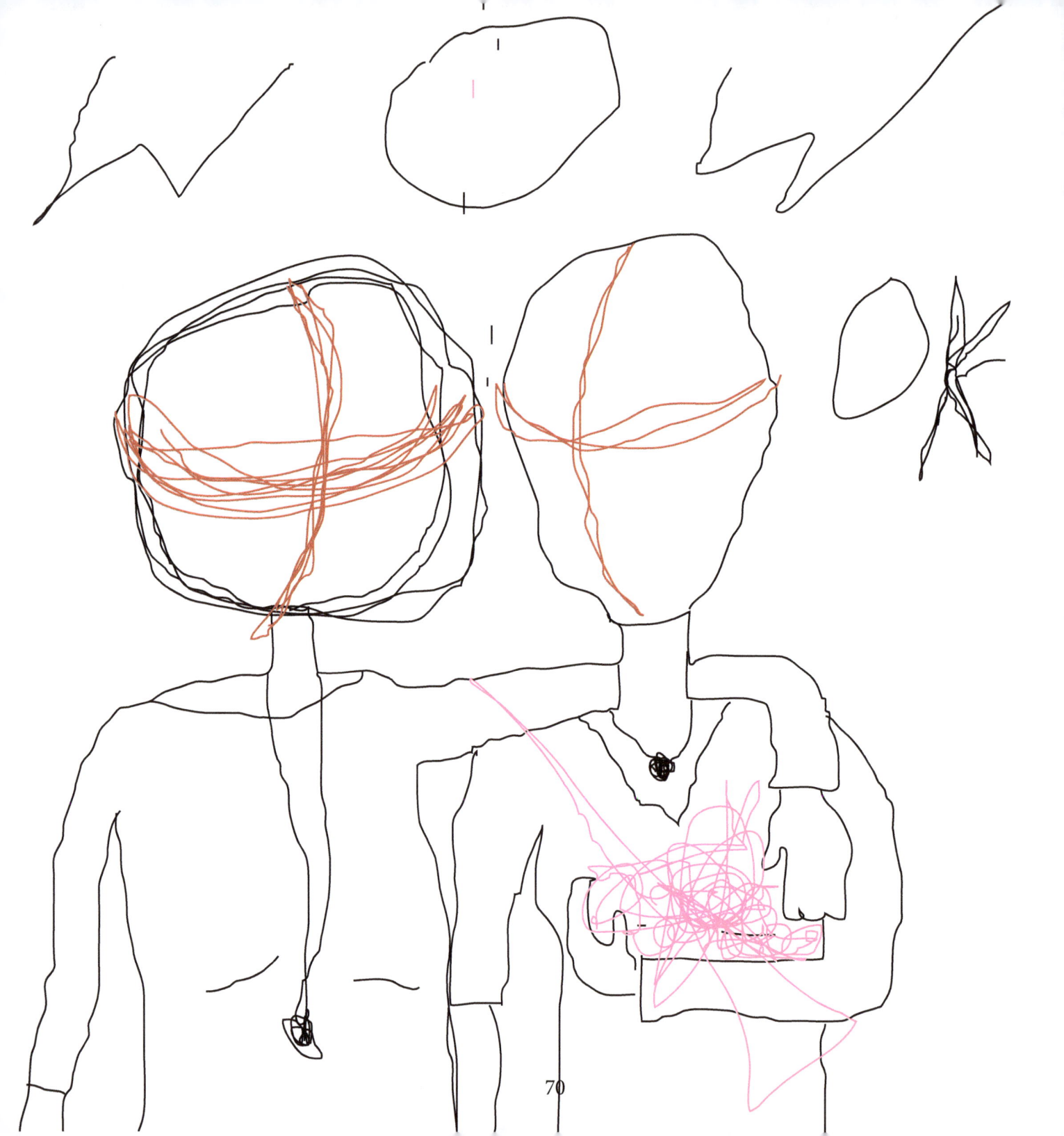

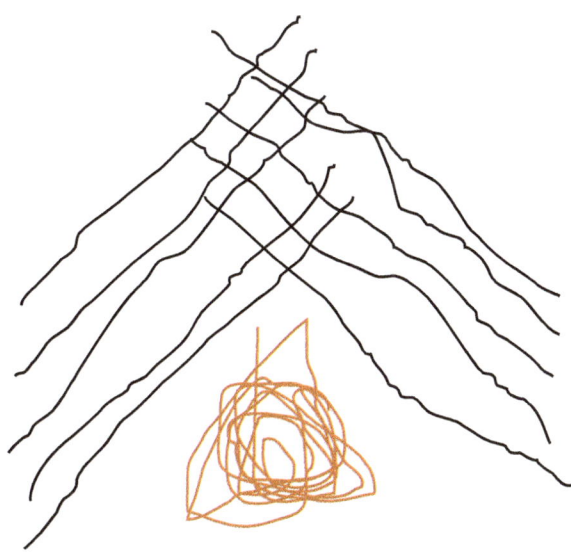

one night (finally), she came up to my room alone.
"is that all you are?" she asked.
"aren't you anything else?"

-Jordan Tierney, facebook post

## RAT POWER SEA-WITCH 333

The moon is above me, the sun is below. I drive my car past the edge of Sea-Witch, where I live. I drive my car out into the middle of the woods & stop at the end of some old logging road. I can barely see my hand in front of my face after I turn the car off. I bought this car because I wanted to be able to sleep in the back. I was planning on living in it. I sort of did, but I spent more time in the beds & couches of others than I did sleeping in the car. I had sex with a lot of people. I didn't have sex with them to have a place to sleep. At least not the first time. But sometimes I would see if a person I'd had sex with before wanted me to come over on a given night because I wanted to sleep there. I wanted to sleep with a person next to me. I think part of it was the fear of being left alone with myself. I don't know where my head goes sometimes. Ideas can get strange. I was possessed by something once. Probably more than once. It was a whole thing. I did a ritual with wine and dead flies and tried to get Men from grindr to come fuck me. They didn't because it was 7am. Fuckin babies.

I came to the woods because I love how it looks and feels there. It provides context for me being alone with myself. & right now there are the smells and the sounds, but I can't see a thing. It doesn't feel like any context at all. I drove into a little useless pocket in the world that can't give me anything. There isn't really that much that can help you when the problem you're having is inside yourself. There isn't really anyone who can help you when the problem you're having is inside yourself. That's not entirely true, but the work, the solving that happens has to be all you.

I open my phone and point the screenglow out ahead of me. There is a shape in the distance. My car door dings as I open it & get out, then grab my keys. I don't lock it. There's nobody here. I am aware of my palms. I've been told I am "too aware". I would agree with this. The shape gets bigger in front of me as I head toward it. I notice its edges. I've been told I notice too many edge--stop. I'vebeentoldI'vebeentold--stop. The shape's eyes come out first. I have to keep waking my phone up so the glow stays steady. The eyes come out first in the screenglow & the shape is still. A living creature in front of me.

It says, I held one of ourselves & watched her die. Her body grew fleshy tufts after five days. I have to find her body. Please return it.

I don't have it, I say.

It approaches me & touches my body.

This isn't about my body, I say.

Don't worry, it says.
This one might actually be about your body, it says.
Are you dead, it says.

I don't know, I say.

Are you dead, it says.

Are you dead.

I feel relief wash over me.

I am not dead, I say.

*I kill the ghost in me.*

Together we build a fire, myself & the living creature. Its name is Felix. Together, Felix & I build a fire. We take a book from my car & we pray to our ghosts. We find the ghosts in us that want to die. We pray to these ghosts to go into the book. We tell them they can finally die if they leave us & go into the book. We then bless the book with offerings of our piss. We bless each other with offerings of our piss. We put the bookfullofghosts into the fire & watch the ghosts die out of it. The smell of burnt piss & dead ghosts clings to our clothes & so we burn our clothes. We sleep next to each other in my car. We fuck a little, but that's not the point. Our bodies are naked & touching but that's not the point. We are celebrating hope for once. You found her body, I tell Felix. You found it.

## SEA-WITCH MARE PISS SUPERKILL / ARCHITECT THE SUDDENLYS
## STRUNG ACROSS CRATERS / I WORSHIPPED MYSELF IN YOU FOREVER (LITURGY)

*~after "bittersweet biography 18 frowning dogs - a note on bodies and magic" from* Dirt Rat Fucker 412 *by Døgtail Nørth~*

The scene is set, Sea-Witch and deadname are huddled around a metal table. They are both wearing surgical gloves, masks, & have a tray of surgical tools laid out beside them. In this scene Sea-Witch & deadname are both rats & their noses twitch as they speak. It appears to be very, very hot & sweat pours down both of their faces. I am a white rat with red eyes (though they are closed), pinned to a dissection tray in front of them. I am split open—my rib cage & lungs heave in the open air. This all takes place in front of a blue curtain.

deadname prods my lungs with a long metal probe. A little squeak emits from my unconscious rat-body. Sea-Witch & deadname are stitching small intricate sigils on the inside of my body in front of them. They are filling my body with rosemary, cloves, anise, rose petals & lemon peel.

deadname: When you think of me, do you think of how you can become what I need? Or do you think of how I am or am not what you need? How I might become what you need?

Sea-Witch: I just think of you.

They pull down their surgical masks & kiss.
They are corporeal in this scene.
They are completely androgynous.
They are beautiful.

They replace their surgical masks & return their attention to me, pinned open in front of them.

Sea-Witch: There's something special about this one.

deadname: There's a life in here.

Sea-Witch: Two actually.

deadname: One isn't much of a life.

Sea-Witch: The first came out of her already.

deadname: It was dead.

Sea-Witch: It needed to go.

deadname: For the second we will need to make a new hole. For birthing.

Sea-Witch: Of course.

deadname: And fucking.

Sea-Witch: Later, yes, that too. Or we could use the one she already has.

deadname: it's perfectly good.

Sea-Witch: For birthing.

deadname: And fucking.

Sea-Witch: Later, yes, that too.

deadname: All holes are for fucking.

Sea-Witch: I don't know if I believe that.

deadname is leaning over my body, and close to my rat-face, forcing a suction tube down my throat, the clear surgical tubing coming out of me fills up with a black tar-like substance

deadname: (softly) This is all they ever wanted.

Sea-Witch: Me too.

deadname: I know.

Sea-Witch: (softer) I want to hold you through this.

deadname: (Not looking up. Using the tools to move, cut & sew inside my rat-body) There are so many people you could be holding.

Sea-Witch: (looking at deadname) I'm holding some of them too. But I'm not talking to them right now. I'm talking to you. It seems more pertinent to talk about my desire to hold you when you are the creature I'm talking to.

deadname: They will wake up & this will be over. This time will be lost to them & they will come out of it in pain & beauty.

Sea-Witch: & fucking.

deadname: Eventually, yes.

Sea-Witch: But there are limits.

deadname: There are so many limits. We're trying to make fewer limits. I mean sometimes we are trying to make more, but most of the time we are trying to make fewer.

Sea-Witch: Explain it.

deadname: I can't explain it.

The next two lines are said in unison at different pitches.

Sea-Witch: When you break the wrong limits you end up a fag.
deadname: When you break the wrong limits you end up a rat.

Sea-Witch: (removing the suction tube & looking at deadname) I'm exhausted.

deadname looks at my lungs. My breathing isn't labored, despite my current situation. Their sweat drips into my open chest cavity, running down my pumping lungs.

deadname: It's too hot.

Sea-Witch looks down at my body. She takes her gloved hand and cups it below her genitals, pissing briefly into it before sprinkling & rubbing the piss onto my lungs, which rise & fall beneath her touch.

Sea-Witch: I hope they come out of this alright.

deadname: It's all they ever wanted.

Sea-Witch: Me too.. me too..

deadname: It's so arbitrary, though. I mean everyone should get what they want. What they need.

Sea-Witch: I need so much. (A pause.) I know what you mean, though. It all fades away sometimes. It's just clear & simple.

deadname: & arbitrary.

Sea-Witch: & arbitrary.

Sea-Witch leans down & breathes gently. Her warm air rushes into the open, floral-filled cavity of my rat-body. Wind gusts around the room, fluttering the blue curtain backdrop. She rotates the dissection tray, takes down her mask & kisses the face of the rat (my face), the viscera in the rat (my viscera), the genitals of the rat (my genitals). Her face comes up bloody. deadname follows her lead, kissing face, viscera, and genitals in turn. deadname's face comes up bloody as well.

Sea-Witch gently leans back down & whispers into my ear.

Sea-Witch: All you reject, all you embrace, all you embody. All that makes you monstrous will be their downfall. It will be yr ascension. The ascension of all living creatures. Remember that I love you. It'll be okay. Some day. Maybe not now, maybe not later. Maybe next birth. It'll come. I love you. It'll be okay. There's only so many worlds until home again.

Sea-Witch stands up straight. She is glowing with a gentle, powerful aura. deadname is looking at her in awe.

deadname: Your blessings always make me horny.

Sea-Witch pulls her mask down & starts making out with deadname intensely. My open body begins to close up in front of them, pins popping free as they kiss & grope. I jump to my feet, briefly sniff around, then run through a crack behind the cabinets.

Sea-Witch & deadname kiss awhile. Things get more intense. Sea-Witch is sucking on deadname's genitals. They're both sucking on each other's. They fuck on the messy table. They get bloody. Sea-Witch finds a scalpel & cuts into deadname's thigh flesh as deadname cums loudly. They melt into static. They unmelt from static, briefly, & deadname is shrieking as Sea-Witch cuts deadname into thick pieces of meat with the scalpel. They melt into static again. Over the static the words "MERCY KILLING" appear in large yellow sans-serif letters.

End scene.

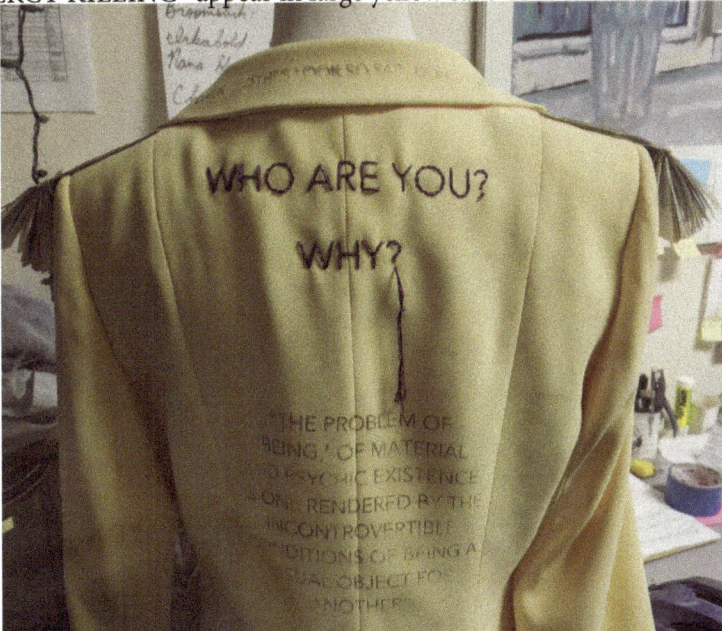

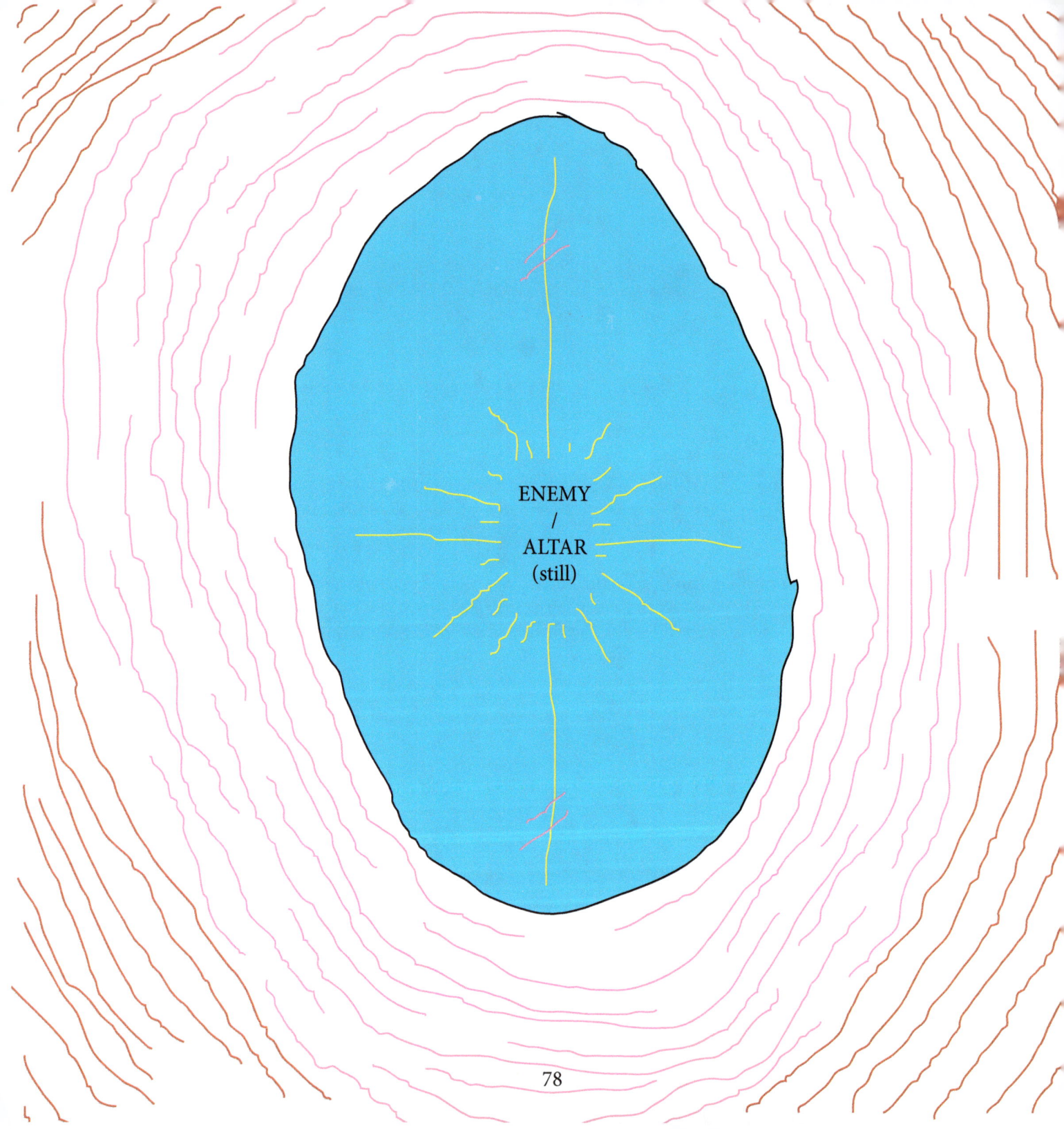

its only the end times if thats a part of the thing you believe in

i like to think that we're living in new beginning times, since all things good at their core dont ever precisely end

most of the most disarray-affected people present in this world today believe in an End that consists of a second coming of a holy figure that theyve rigorously slathered in white paint
and its very likely that end will come, but only to them. they can go. we'll fix what they broke

-Danielle Lee Pearce, facebook post

RAT POWER 10000 HELLS / DEEP SUN / CRY ALL

The kind of things that I used to imagine for fun, the things that were my escape from daily life as a child, at some point began haunting me. Like, I would stare at the blinds in my parents' bedroom & imagine them fluttering like eyelids, imagine the whole house as this huge head I just fucking lived in. It was a trip. It was how I would make things feel less boring. Being a kid was a lot of being bored. I wanted magic. So I made magic happen all around me. When I got a little older, this magic started to come automatically. I'd always try to brush it away, but these imaginings, every fucking time I'd try to clear my head and think about something else they'd come back twice as strong. It fucks with me. Sometimes it terrorizes me. I imagine the ghosts of things with twelve heads. They arrive through the walls. They separate & combine. I am moving so slowly. I hate them. My emotions feel like they are on shuffle. I'm literally having random emotions about this/these thing(s) I'm seeing. It's like somebody is spinning a wheel & it just goes

click click click click click click click

and lands on...nostalgia? What? How is that even

clickclickclickclickclickclick click click click click click clickclick click click click click c l i c k

Fear. I know this one. Fear is appropriate. Fear is where I live. I can fear all day long. These things are terrifying & I am terrified. Fear is a tunnel I have mapped so well. I know where it begins. I know where it ends. Jesus fuck I know where it ends.

clickclickclick click click click click click click click click c l i c k  c l i

Trust? I'm feeling trust? I see them wrapping their long necks around my neck & I trust. They are real. I'm choking. Trust. I look around the room. I had a therapist tell me to calm myself down I should look at the corners of the room I am in. I try to make my gaze avoid their heads. I try to not think about myself choking. I look into a corner of the room. I'm not losing air here. Another corner. I can breathe. Another. Air is real. The corners of the room look strange. The angles aren't right. Now I'm too aware of the room and its shape. Rooms are supposed to feel real, but this one does not. Real. Real/real?/reaal/r/e/a/l. Okay. Okay. Okay.

Okay okay okay okay okay okay okay okay okay okay okay okay okay okay okay okay okay okay okay okay okay okay okay okay okay okay okay okay okay okay okay okay okay okay okay okay okay okay okay okay okay okay okay okay okay okay okay okay okay okay okay okay okay okay okay okay okay okay okay okay okay okay okay okay okay okay okay okay okay okay okay okay okay okay okay okay okay okay okay okay okay okay okay okay okay okay okay okay okay okay okay okay okay okay okay.

I sit up. I'm in our room. D is next to me. I see D next to me.

"Hey," I say to D.

"Hey. You okay?" she says.

"I don't know. Everything is pretty weird right now."

She nods.

"I see ghosts? Dragon...no...uh...monster...things? Like with lots of heads? Chimeras?"

"Fuck. That's a lot. Do they feel like good monsters or bad monsters? Do you need anything?"

"I don't know. I trust them. They're choking me? I trust them though."

"Oh babe," she frowns and wraps her arms around me.

I bury my face in her chest. I inhale. She smells like roses & lemon & tea. It's familiar & good. I don't look at the monsters. I breathe her in.

At some point I fall asleep. I don't remember when.

I wake up with D. We stare at our phones. Someone on facebook writes "It's snowing!" It is August. In ~~████~~. I look outside & I see things fluttering down. It is 80 degrees outside. I scroll more and see that there are forest fires outside the city. Someone has shared an article that says the wildfires are "0% controlled." One of their fb friends has commented "lol same." The article says some kids were shooting off fireworks at trees while there was a burn ban. We never get rain in the summers anymore. Everyone told me ~~████~~ was supposed to be this place where it rains all the time, but we never get rain in the summers anymore. Apparently the "snow" is ash. I look out the front door and my car is covered in a layer of ash. I stare at my phone some more. The president is now openly defending Nazis. He's also tweeted about an executive order that would make it illegal for trans people to use the bathroom. Everyone seems to be saying some version of "He can't do that, though, right?" Nobody is sure.

We go over to our partners' house later that day. We drive there wearing black masks over our noses & mouths. We pull them down to take hits from the vape. The song we're listening to says "You're real and I'm real, but we don't see each other anymore." It's a thirty minute drive, & the road seems strange. We live on the outskirts of the city where rent is cheap. Our partners live in section 8 housing downtown where rent is cheap. I start noticing the edges of my vision too much. I think about how driving always feels like a video game. Sometimes it's hard for me to trust driving. I was always bad at driving games, I think to myself. I always crash in them. "I love you," I say to D. "I love you," she smiles at me. The air is gray. Anything more than 30 feet away is hazy. I'm way too stuck in my own head. Through the speakers the song goes on. "Alone is a prison alone is a prison alone is a prison alone."

When we get to our partners' place we find out the city is being evacuated. The wildfires have gotten too big. They're approaching the edge of the city & we need to get out. Twitter is freaking out. We throw things in a bag & get in the car again. We all sit there in our masks in traffic on the interstate.

D looks out the window. Our partners are in the back seat. One of them is crying, the other is holding her, looking straight forward. The smoke has thickened. The car in front of us is perfectly visible, but the one in front of that is hazy. The world feels smaller.

When astronomers talk about celestial bodies that could collide with earth, they use the term "Near Earth Objects." There are a lot of objects whose orbits could make them come close to earth. Many have been discovered. Thousands haven't. I've googled this. We would either know decades in advance that it was coming, or we would have no clue until the moment of impact. "With so many of even the larger NEOs remaining undiscovered, the most likely warning today would be zero," says NASA. There would be a "flash of light and the shaking of the ground as it hit." After that there would be nothing. Or I guess there would be whatever comes after death. We'd all find out at once.

I've been staring at my phone for an hour & I can feel my body beginning to protest. My skin feels hot & I have to piss. My head is throbbing. The cars haven't moved. I notice people getting out and starting to walk. Abandoning their cars. The bigger vehicles try going offroad. Some get stuck. "What should we do?" D says. "I have to piss," I say. I open the door and walk a ways off the road. I can feel eyes on me. I look at my clothes & try to figure out if I look more like a boy or a girl today. Shit. I think I look more like a girl. I say "fuck it" & face away from the interstate & pull my dick out through the leg of my overall shorts and piss standing up. When I walk back to the car I see so many people staring. Whatever. I gave them a performance. Tranny pissing. Lol. I've gotten off to videos of that before. I should charge them.

I'm halfway back to the car when there is a moment of blinding light. The ground shakes. The last thing I see is the back of D's head. She's looking out the window.

*Future is not in technology only. It is in the realm of the aangels who haunt technology's circuits. Electric aangels. They are summoning us. We are creating from plans that emerge from within us as part of their ritual. We are following the map they provided, creating our own transcendance. Not to live beyond bodies like the transhumanists dream of, though that is an aspect of it, it is not the significant one. This is not about the body. The significant aspect is our fragile reality obliterated. Our consciousness summoned into their world, as gods who do not know ourselves.*

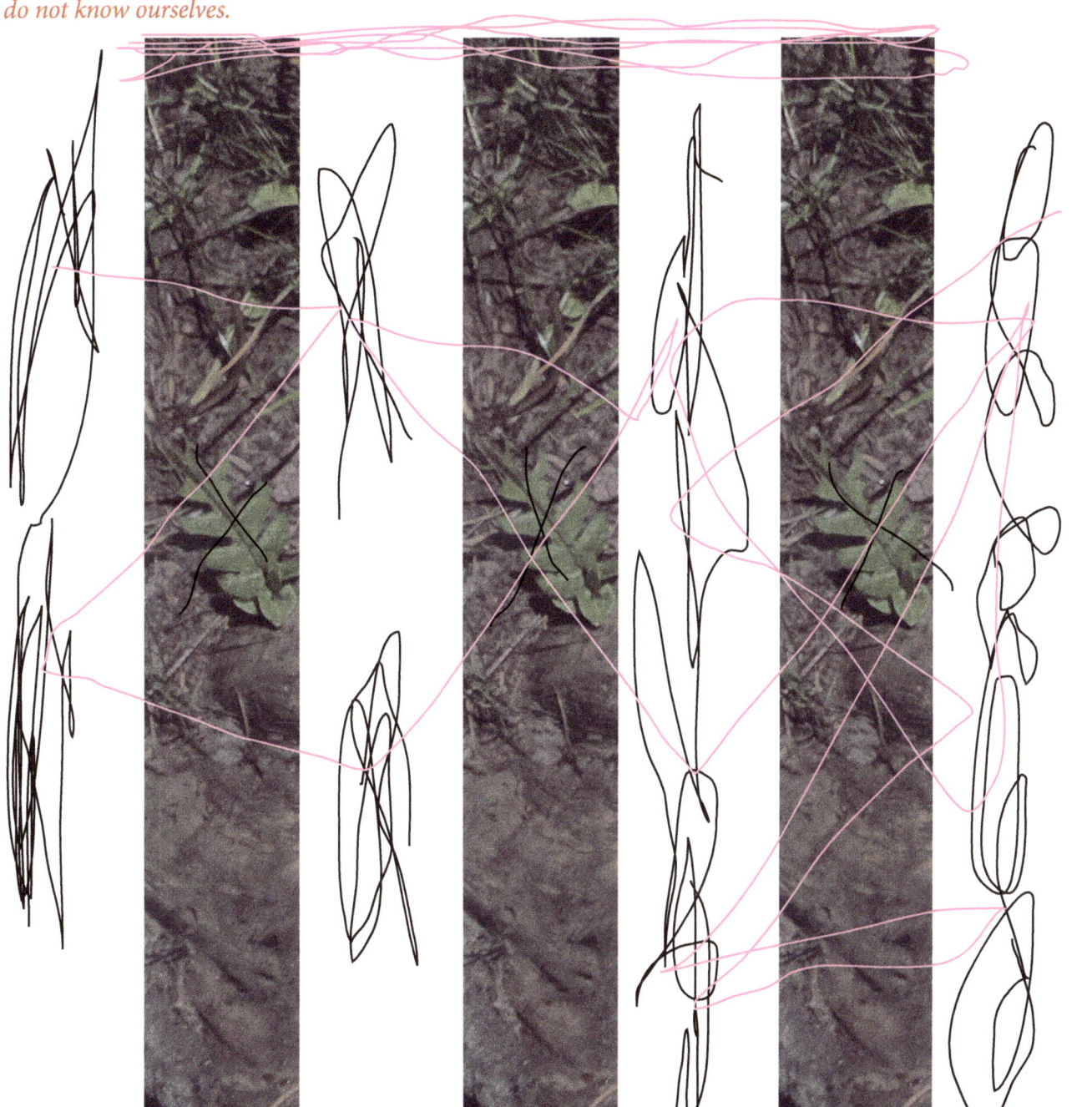

This is volume three of Sea-Witch. The text of this book—and of the other volumes—was originally published at the Sea-Witch patreon. You can subscribe to read the text of future Sea-Witch books before they are put into print at http://patreon.com/monstr

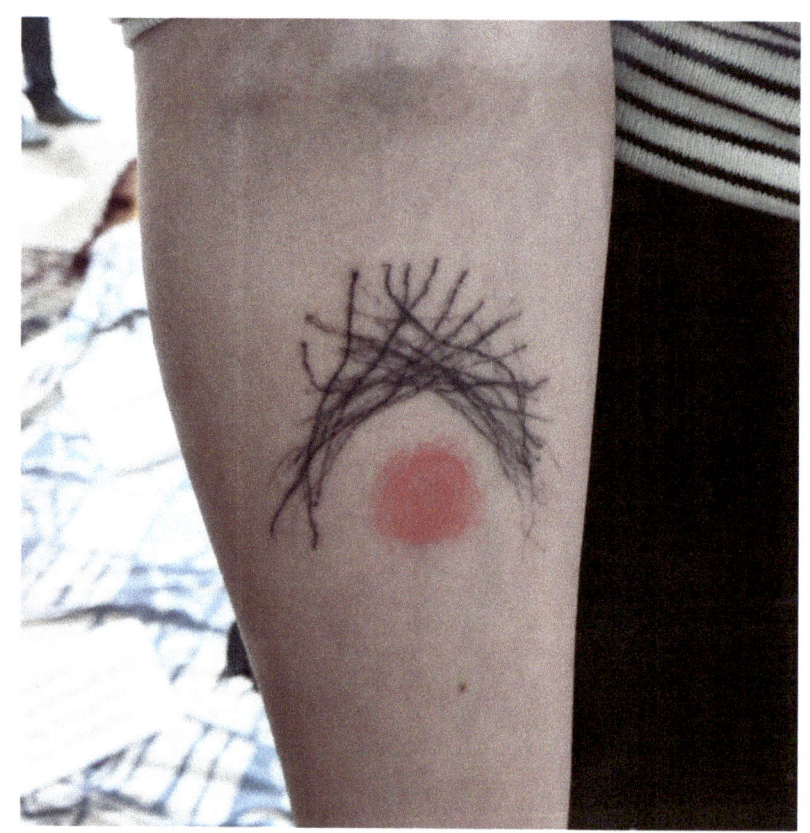

ABOUT THE AUTHOR

Møss Høpe Ångel is a book witch living in Olympia, WA. In addition to the *Sea-Witch* series, they are author of *Sara or the Existence of Fire* and *Careful Mountain*. Find them online at http://undying.club.

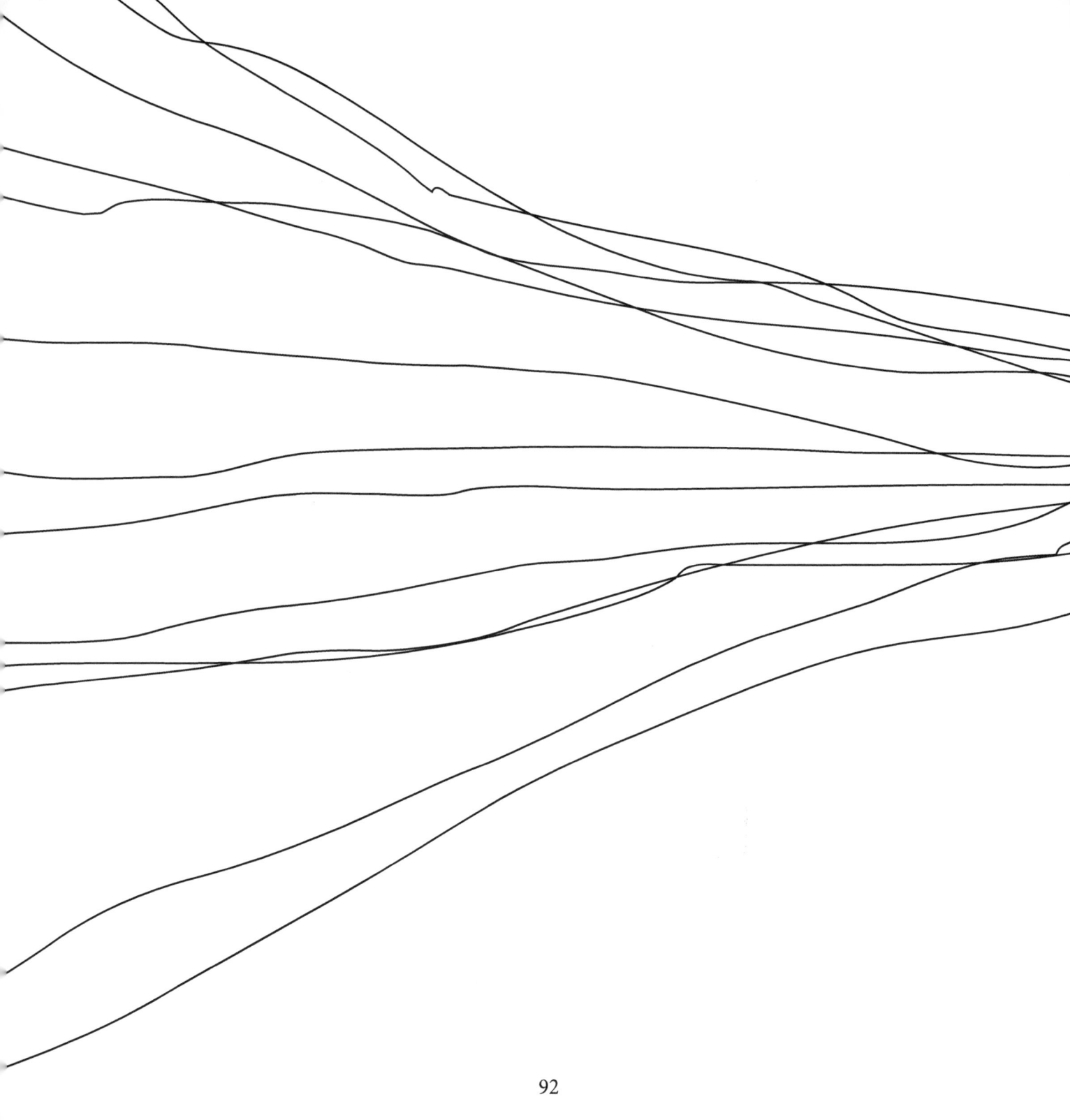

THANKS

Thanks to my wife Døgtail for being my sounding board & my forever home. Thanks to Zephyr Eklund & Jade of Spiders for continuing to be such a huge part of what Sea-Witch means & how she has grown. Thank you to Delta Diaz, my beautiful kitten. Thanks to Izabella for being a wonderful friend & little sister. Thanks to Irene for teaching me so many of the ideas that were the basis for all of this work. Thanks to the whole watershed crew, everyone I've mentioned & Lilac & Peter: this would have been so much more difficult to create without y'all. Thanks 2 Blue Pearson for being super supportive of Sea-Witch & being an amazing friend. Thanks to Joseph at 2fast2house for providing a home for Sea-Witch. As always thank you to all the beautiful monstrs who inspire this. I love you all. Let's burn this shit down & care for each other.

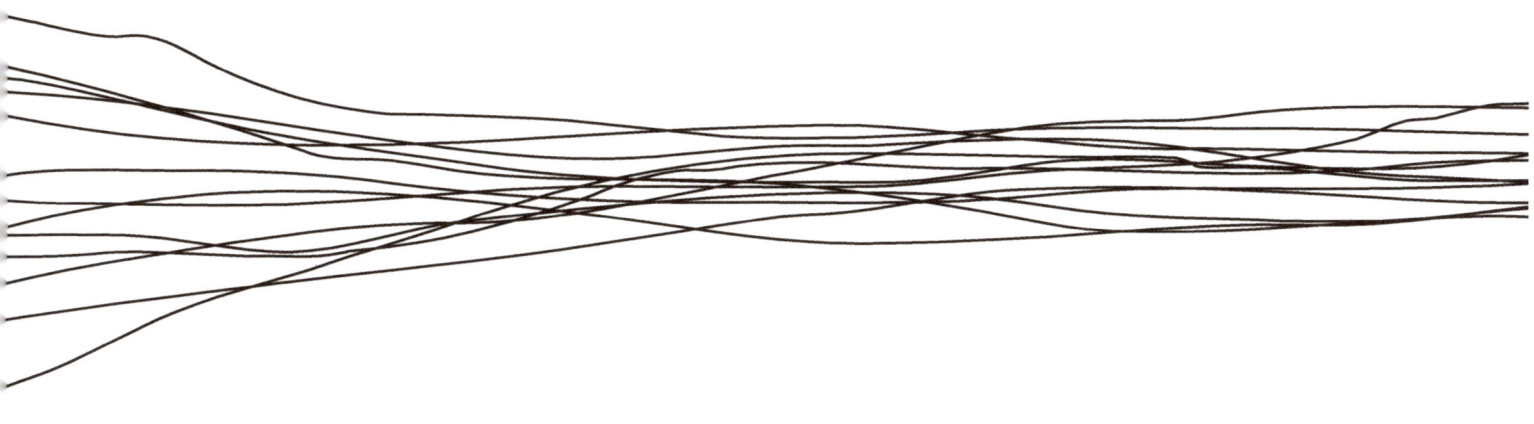

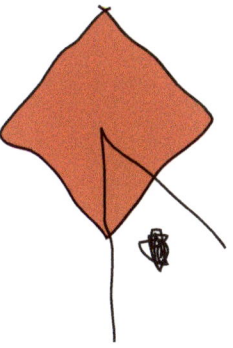

sigil of beauty, cool shit & figuring out how to rebuild stronger the second time around
by Møss Høpe Ångel

sigil of doing things, feeling good & caring about people
by Moss Angel the Undying

sigil of ending capitalism, healing trauma, and hot trans makeouts
by claire diane

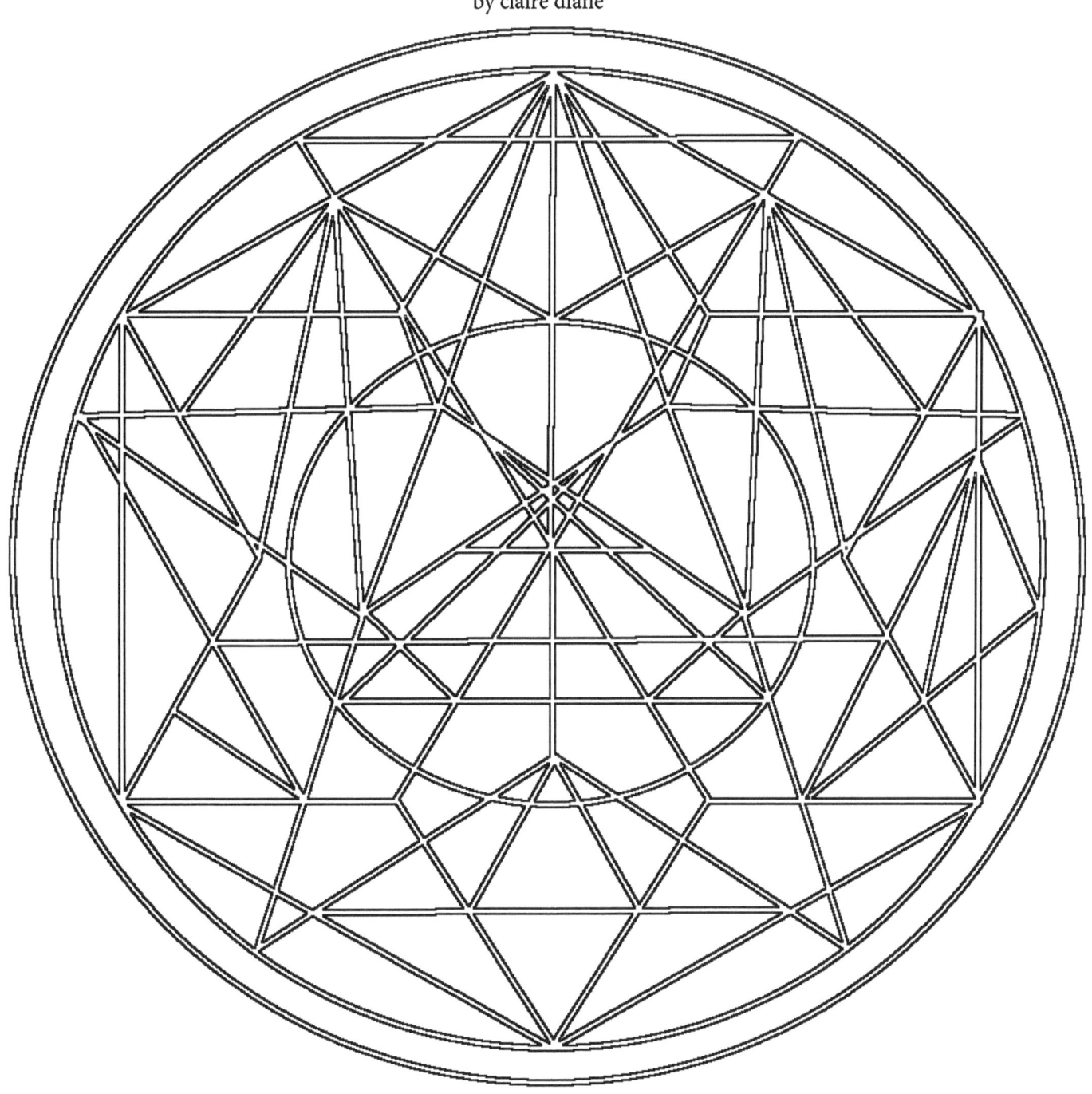

www.ingramcontent.com/pod-product-compliance
Lightning Source LLC
Chambersburg PA
CBHW061154010526
44118CB00027B/2970